THOUGHTS ON JUDAISM

LILY H. MONTAGU

Published by Left of Brain Books

Copyright © 2021 Left of Brain Books

ISBN 978-1-396-32094-1

First Edition

All rights reserved. No part of this publication may be reproduced, distributed, or transmitted in any form or by any means, including photocopying, recording, or other electronic or mechanical methods, without the prior written permission of the publisher, except in the case of brief quotations embodied in critical reviews and certain other noncommercial uses permitted by copyright law. Left of Brain Books is a division of Left of Brain Onboarding Pty Ltd.

Table of Contents

INTRODUCTION	1
CHAPTER I	4
CHAPTER II	9
CHAPTER III	14
CHAPTER IV	22
CHAPTER V	28
CHAPTER VI	35
CHAPTER VII	39
CHAPTER VIII	50
CHAPTER IX	58

INTRODUCTION

THIS little book purposes to explain my conception of Judaism as a living religion. In endeavouring to answer the questions–What are the vital principles of Judaism? Why are they vital? How can they be applied to modern life?—I have ventured to reveal my own faith, for the experience of one soul, however unimportant in itself, may serve as a testimony to the living faith which is among us. Clearly there can be, on my part, no claim to any authority whatever; nor do I pretend that my conception of Judaism is novel. It owes a great deal to Mr Montefiore's essay on "Liberal Judaism," though the point of view is not everywhere the same. But, like Mr Montefiore, I too have ventured to work on constructive lines, and to give, however briefly and imperfectly, a personal presentment of Judaism. I have written in a dogmatic strain, not assuredly because I am not painfully conscious of my own limitations, but because there is a large body of Jews who require the construction, at any rate in outline, of a definite theory of their faith. They are anxious to realise and to transmit Judaism as a living faith, but have no time or inclination to work out the principles and deductions of such a faith for themselves. This class includes busy men and women who "have enough to do already without thinking very much about their religion." There are others who think Judaism all right in its proper place, but do not believe it affects *them* more often, perhaps, than two or three times a year. They cherish certain prejudices which belonged to their parents, and when they attend synagogue, are glad that it should recall memories of their infancy. Therefore they resist the bogey of "reform," but their religion has merely an impersonal interest. It makes no demands on their lives; it is no real help to them. Then there are the parents who want their children to be faithful to Judaism, but cannot see how they can attach them to a doctrine, which appears to them to be obsolete. There are the conscientious teachers who long to make their lessons alive and interesting, but who themselves have not yet *quite* assimilated the spiritual strength which they would transmit. All these people seem to feel that Judaism, without dogma, is too shadowy a faith to be really acceptable to them. There is also that large section of Jews who, like myself, are seeking to understand the value of their spiritual inheritance, and who may feel sympathy with some of my conclusions.

I have tried to remember the point of view of these various classes, and in a practical manner to satisfy some of their needs. My effort may perhaps stimulate others in the same direction, and with better results. Thus points of religious agreement rather than differences are emphasised, and it is proved that the same Ideal of Righteousness inspires all sections of our community. The variety of conceptions held by believing Jews, are at once a peril and a blessing to Judaism. For what are the reasons for this variety? In the first place, since the authority for our creed rests in human conscience, its phases must be as varied as individuality itself. Secondly, Judaism has always been closely connected with life, and life becomes more complex as civilisation develops.

Judaism is the hallowing of existing ideals, and ideals shift from generation to generation. A religion which rests on conscience is a robust religion, and makes a supreme demand on all human faculties. It claims the highest life from its devotees. The close connection between religion and life is clearly the ideal which all cults emphasise. How then is the variety a peril? It gives an excuse to the indifferent to devote their minds to other causes, instead of attempting to realise the principles of Judaism. They argue that a religion which depends on the conscience of each individual, is the concern of each individual, and if he chooses to neglect it, his apathy need not trouble his neighbours. If he wishes, he can adopt a more convenient faith, or, if he is thoroughly indolent, he can say, "Since there are so many conceptions none can be entirely true. I will not trouble myself but will drift on to the end of my life and be comfortable." I have tried to show that indifference is a malignant growth which leads to spiritual destruction, and that its influence spreads far beyond the life of any individual sufferer. It is dangerous to feel too comfortable about religious matters, for this sort of comfort generally prevents aspiration. We are here to struggle nearer to the divine truth and goodness. We shall not get very far if our ideal is *comfort*, if we merely want to cover up our indifference instead of fighting and overcoming it. The "building-up time" has arrived, and I venture to appeal to all who sympathise with my religious conception, to help in the work of reconstruction. We must rouse the indifferent from their lethargy and get them to realise their religious obligations. Each community must contribute some vitality to the religious ideal of its own generation.

The beauty of Judaism is useless unless we can consciously assimilate it in our lives. Before it can be assimilated it must be understood. This book attempts to explain, as definitely and clearly as possible, the meaning of our faith as it appears to one Jewish believer.[1]

---

[1] In this connection I wish to express my sincere thanks to Mr and Mrs C. G. Montefiore for the sympathy and encouragement they have given me throughout the production of my book, and for their practical suggestions for its improvement. Had it not been for their help I should have been overwhelmed by the difficulty of making myself articulate. While acknowledging most gratefully my indebtedness to these friends, I would remind my readers that I alone am responsible for the many limitations and imperfections of my work.

CHAPTER I

MOST of us are agreed that certain principles are vital to Judaism. By this we mean that Judaism as a religion could not exist if any one of these principles were refuted. We believe that they cannot be refuted, and we endeavour, as far as we can, to reveal this faith through our lives. Quite apart from the accident of our birth, quite apart from our fidelity to ceremonials, we claim to belong to the Jewish brotherhood, because we accept the following principles as eternal truths:–

I. *There is one sole Creator or God.*
This great central fact dominates all our religious conceptions. Biblical prophets and teachers did not speculate very frequently on the nature of God. They were surrounded by nations who put their trust in many gods, and made material representations of them for purposes of worship. This idolatry, originating as it did in a variety of causes, may have been partly stimulated by a deep sense of reverence. The world seemed so wonderful to these primitive worshippers, that it was impossible for them to believe that it could all have been the work of one God. So they divided up the dominion of nature and placed it under many rulers. Gradually they attributed all sorts of coarse human passions to these various gods, and consequently the worship of them became degraded and impure. Then was the idea of God's unity revealed to the Jewish prophets and thinkers, and at the same time they recognised their own human limitations. They *were not meant* to understand His being, they were only called upon to recognise and pay homage to the attributes by which He makes Himself manifest to His creatures. These teachers were filled with awe at the greatness and power of God, and with gratitude for His love. They denounced with all their strength the creation of idols, since idolatry degraded worship. The one God was manifest in all His works; any effort to symbolise His power could only limit His greatness, which was infinite. To-day we have not any temptation to make idols. Common sense shows us the absurdity of such worship as belonged to the child period of the world's history. When we

declare our faith in the Unity of God, we mean primarily that the Ruler of the Universe is one, and that His very nature forms a unity. In Him there is no clashing of wills or varieties of purpose. As He was, so He is and so He will be, and by His high and changeless will the universe is governed and controlled. Secondly, we mean that God is "pure" spirit, for singleness of nature is implied in unity, and we can only conceive what we call "soul," or spirit as absolutely *one* and changeless. Thirdly, we mean that, in our belief, the one spirit is revealed in all forms of creation; that the one Spiritual Being is omnipresent. To Him belong perfect love, truth and beauty, and these attributes are manifest in His works.

II. From the belief in God's existence and unity important consequences follow. The second vital principle embodied in Judaism is *"That the God of the World has relations with each human soul, and that each soul, being an emanation from Him, must be, like Him, immortal."* Our faith in the perfect oneness of God involves our faith that the human spirit, in however infinitesimal a degree, shares His attributes. Because God is immortal, the spirit with which He has animated us cannot be liable to decay.

We can recognise two important channels, through which the divine life works in the spiritual world. The all-powerful, all-loving God, who has called all creation into being, can influence and sustain every form of life. The human spirit can, through communion with God, renew its strength from the divine source whence it came. God in His love has given us the supreme gift of aspiration. In seeking to lead a higher life, we open our hearts to receive strength from God. Our Father in His pity and love reaches down to us and helps us. We, in our efforts to lead better lives, move a little nearer to God.

The power of communion between man and God is revealed in the influence of love on our lives. We are conscious of God's love, when we cease to vex our souls with harassing questions and miserable self-absorption, when we stand still and look up. Then we are at peace and we feel God's presence. Then again, pure, unselfish human love spiritualises our lives, inasmuch as it is in spired by the God who is the source of love. In its purity and beauty it reflects, however remotely, the glory of God. Life under the influence of love becomes bright with possibilities which stretch beyond and above the world of passion and sordid struggle. Love unites us to the God of life. In experiencing love we know ourselves immortal.

III. The Unity of God involves the existence of law. God governs the world by law. When the leaves fall off the trees in autumn, we are sure that the vital sap is being secreted and that the joyous beauty of spring will follow the dreary barrenness of winter. That is God's law. When at the seaside, we see the tide ebb and the sand appear, we know that this condition will not last. There will be high tide again at the exact moment when we expect it. We know God's immutable law. These physical laws, which belong to a group known as the laws of nature, are not the only laws which, because of their immutability, we can call God's laws. There is also the moral law, upon which another Jewish principle is founded. *We are responsible to God for our conduct, and if we sin we must bear the consequences of our sin. No intercessor is possible or necessary between man and God. The Divine love enters into the hearts of those who seek it with prayer and contrition.* Every created being is meant to develop the law of its existence, to develop all its powers and to live a full live. Human beings are endowed with certain powers of mind, and heart, and body, which, being *good* must belong to the one Divine Being, Who in His oneness includes all things good. We have the power to be good—to realise the spiritual life which is the best in us. We are endowed with the power to know evil and to reject it. When we turn away from goodness and choose evil, we slip away from God, and life becomes difficult and harassing. Only through repentance and a changed life can the soul which sin has separated from God feel near to Him again. We bear the pain of isolation when we sin. There can be no union with God except through righteousness, for the nature of God is entirely good.

But while conscious of our sin, we are also conscious of the power of reuniting ourselves with God. If we will only repent, and by continuous effort improve our lives, we can atone for our sin and realise again the peace which comes from God. Sin cannot be linked to goodness. The two are distinct—apart, eternally separate. No intercessory power can obtain for us remission of our sins. We have the power to make atonement for ourselves. We can turn from our sin and again live at one with God. When we sin we separate ourselves from God. But He, being eternal in His wisdom and His love, does not lose sight of us. He knows us still, even when we sin. He knows our weakness and our temptation. His love *must* be beautified by pity—for how otherwise could He in His perfection love us? When we turn from our sin, when we recognise it and hate it, and allow ourselves to suffer the pain of remorse, our nature is purified and spiritualised. The divine love enters into our hearts. We have atoned; we are at one. The more frequent the sin, the more terrible the separation, the more difficult the return. We can imagine people who form the habit of evil-doing, lose consciousness of the power of this Divine love. They slip further and further from the source of pure happiness, and in this separateness they experience the consequences of sin.

IV. When we become conscious of the love of God, as revealed in our own lives, we feel instinctively drawn to our neighbours, who share with us the spiritual life which is divine. *The love of our neighbours is then a necessary development of our love of God.* His unity is revealed in the oneness of the human family, in their common need—the need for love. We dare not shrink from any fellow-being, seeing that we are all the children of God. Obviously, then, we can only fulfil the law of our being and realise a full life if we develop the power of service. In helping our neighbours we are revealing our love for God; we are doing homage to His unity.

These four vital principles of Judaism are embodied in our "Shema"—the prayer which should be the inspiration of our lives. In this prayer we declare the Unity of God and proclaim our allegiance to the law of love—that love which should purify our conduct in all its various phases. It is by love we reach God; it is through love that we avoid sin; it is through love that we seek to accomplish our duty to our neighbours and to posterity.

V. If we reflect on the spiritual possibilities of life, inspired by the principles of Judaism, we cannot doubt *that the Jewish brotherhood exists for a definite religions purpose.* We are the guardians of a perfectly pure religious idea, for we are the direct descendants of those men who, in an age of idolatry and degradation, bore witness to the Unity of God. We have been taught by generations of believers that God is the God of righteousness, and that by righteousness alone can He be served. If we are to be true to the charge which our fathers have laid upon us, we must hand down to our children this pure faith. And we must transmit it not only by the declaration of our lips, but also by the example of our lives. God has allowed Israel to survive all the terrors of ignorance, persecution, self-indulgence and superstition, in order that we may bear witness to the power of faith as a hallowing of life. If we can only realise the privilege and joy of this work, we shall be equal to the efforts of self-realisation and self-sacrifice which it demands. It is because we are often such unwilling and unfaithful witnesses, that the vitalising power of Judaism is so little recognised by the world. When Israel knows its God and allows love to glorify its life, other nations join with it in a common worship. On that day will the Lord be one and name one.

CHAPTER II

IN the previous chapter I have given my conception of the vital principles of Judaism. In the following pages I propose to explain this conception more fully.

It is obviously impossible to prove the existence of God. We ask ourselves—On what evidence do we base our faith? How, in the face of so much misery and evil, can we believe in an all-powerful, all-merciful and all-just God? Our replies will only satisfy our fellow-believers. We do not pretend to satisfactorily "explain" God by processes of reasoning and by argument, for we know the limitations of the human intellect.

We believe that "God's thoughts are not our thoughts and our ways are not His ways." We see evidence around us of the existence of law, and we worship God as the author of law. In man there is abundant evidence of the spiritual life. Acts of pure self-sacrifice and of noble heroism cannot be explained on physical grounds. The very incompleteness of the noblest human lives, the suffering of the "finite heart that yearns," the endless striving after unattainable ideals, all bear testimony to the existence of a God Whose perfection inspires mortals with a "divine discontent."

We feel God's presence within ourselves and in the good desires which sometimes obtain a mastery over our lives and force us to accomplish deeds of love. The finite mind cannot comprehend the Infinite—the imperfect spirit fails utterly, when it seeks to measure itself with Perfection. But God can satisfy the souls of those who seek Him. He can make himself felt. We can solve the secret of the Lord when we fear Him. No amount of logical exposition can explain the certainty or the intensity of our faith. We feel God and are at rest. We seek not to understand Him for we realise that none of us shall "see His face and live."

It seems clear that *experience* alone can convince us of the existence of God, of His love for righteousness, of His relations to each human soul. To the sceptic, who cannot admit the possibility of God's Fatherhood, we can only say, "Pray, ask God to reveal Himself to you, accept the limitations of your understanding, throw yourself on God's mercy, speak to Him your doubts, and then 'stand in awe and sin not, commune with your heart upon your bed and be still.'" This silent waiting is difficult to achieve in our age of disquietude and of restless activity. We toss about one philosophical theory after another and can get no rest. But, if we will only be still, we shall bear the word, "very nigh to us in our minds and in our hearts, that we may do it." When we peer into the future and consider certain troubles which may overtake us, we are sometimes inclined to believe that such troubles will be quite intolerable; we shall succumb under their burden. But God reveals Himself in many ways, and sometimes the whisper of His love is most clearly heard in the midst of tribulation. To Hagar, as she watched in the wilderness, came the voice of God bidding her arise and shake off her agony and take up her child and live. The mother-love revealed in Hagar lives to-day in all its passionate intensity, and noble purity, and reflects, in spite of human frailty, some of the brightest rays of the divine love—the rays of pity, tenderness, unselfishness and forgiveness. Yet how often in our own experience do we see this mother-love overtaken by the most overwhelming trials. A child is snatched away without warning by some swift malady another is seen to linger in suffering, and the remedies which would relieve the pain are beyond the mother's means—she must watch the suffering and cry aloud in her impotence. Nothing avails—God's will is done. Another child, full of bright promise, is chained to a life of misery and temptation. The mother-love is in conflict with conditions which it cannot overthrow, even though through its intensity it survives in their despite. In all these instances, we bow our heads in awe before the mystery of God's love. According to the beautiful Maccabæan legend, the oil which seemed only sufficient for the one night's ritual celebrations in the Temple fed the sacred lamp for a whole week. Similarly, our power, which seems so limited, is in times of trial strengthened by God's love. He never sends us trouble without supplying us at the same time with the courage to endure. But we must train ourselves to seek His help—to look up in prayer to His throne. Then when the moment of our trouble comes, our faith will not fail us. The glorious light of hope and love will burst through the darkest clouds and irradiate once more our lives. We cannot go through life without learning to know and to admire men and women, who bear their troubles with splendid fortitude, who live saintly lives, but who nevertheless deny that they are in any way conscious of the existence of God. Our acquaintance with these heroic men and women sometimes affects us uncomfortably. We are mystified by their courage, and their scepticism suggests doubts to ourselves. But there is no question that many of these sceptics love and worship God under a name which they create for themselves. Perhaps they believe in goodness, or in law, or in nature, or in a spiritual essence, and consciously or unconsciously endow these abstractions with many of the attributes which, according to Jewish teaching, belong to God. But we must admit that there are others who serve God by their righteousness, while yet unable to acknowledge His sovereignty. They are strong enough to live good lives without the aids to holiness, which religion supplies. But while reverencing these courageous folk, and admitting that their righteousness makes our lapses all the more grievous and shameful, we venture, nevertheless, to believe that the possibilities of virtue must be greater to the believer than to the unbeliever. "Life's ideals are hallowed by religion," and if we refuse to recognise the existence of perfection outside our lives, we must admit limitations to the degree of our own endeavour. Moreover, the strong man who relies solely on his strength cannot live free from peril. Hillel taught us never to be sure of ourselves till the day of our death. Further, none of us can live for ourselves alone. The sceptic, like every other man since the days of Cain, is destined to be his brother's keeper. He is responsible for his children, and even for his neighbours, whom he may have infected with his scepticism. Who knows whether their strength will be equal to his own? It is the task of the believing Jew to wage a crusade against religious indifference, and negation, with all their deadening tendencies. His effective weapon will be the testimony of a holy life illuminated by joy and hope and dignified by responsibility and purpose.

Our belief in the immortality of the soul rests primarily on our faith in God's Unity[2] and can be further explained by our consciousness of His love. We have been endowed with powers of mind and heart which we cannot fully realise in this world. Human love would be indeed an irony if it ended with death. Our desire to learn wisdom, to work righteousness, to attain pure joy, can never be completely satisfied on earth. These desires are good; they come

---

[2] *See* page 5, par. II.

from God; they testify to our immortality, for the God who sent them loves us and will not suffer any good thing to be lost.

Unless we can accept as a vital principle of our faith the fact that the love of our fellow-men is a necessary development of our love for God, domestic and social life lose their sanctity. If the service of man is a form of divine service, passion and self-interest cannot tempt us to deny our domestic and civic obligations. Moreover, in reverencing the unity of God as revealed in His creation, we are ready to work without reward to brighten lives yet unborn.

When Frederic William of Prussia ordered his chaplain to prove in one sentence the truth of religion, he answered, "The Jews, Your Majesty!" This story cannot fail to gratify our vanity, but it should also quicken our sense of responsibility. The Jews continued to exist through ages of sorrow, ignorance and persecution. They preserved the holy purity of their faith in spite of all temptations and misfortunes. It was difficult enough to remain faithful, to resist the temptation of perjury. Again and again they could have bought comfort and advancement for themselves and for their children by denying the faith which they had inherited. But they remained true. They declared their allegiance to God and their faith in His love and in the claims of personal service. But they did not step at mere verbal declaration. If they had not shown that their faith in God inspired righteous conduct, that it affected their common everyday life, then no inspiring lesson could be drawn from their survival. But throughout the ages the Jews believed in God and this belief affected their conduct. They were at peace although they were surrounded by deadly foes; God satisfied all their highest longings, although they lived in penury; and they were free in the midst of their bondage, because they believed themselves to be both the servants and the children of God.

To-day, in England, we are surrounded by different temptations. Life is easier; the roads to prosperity and success are open to us. Our needs are less obvious and crude than those of past generations; nevertheless, the obligation to praise God is less easily remembered than that of petitioning Him. Prosperity seems to have dulled our sense of gratitude instead of quickening it, and to have increased our greed. Perhaps, also, the importance of declaring our faith in the one God is less apparent since other communities have proclaimed their allegiance to Him. But surely life can never be easy to live *well*. We stumble forward and new rocks are in our path. We look into the future and new opportunities of service influence our imagination. As we go forward we need light and yet more light, and this light can be supplied by our faith. As we, with our improved opportunities, grow in intellectual and moral power, our faith should grow in intensity. A religion is dead unless it can satisfy the needs of a progressing civilisation.

We claim that Judaism embodies vital and eternal principles which can in all ages lead men to righteousness. Unless we believe ourselves to be the appointed guardians of these truths, we shall not be able to resist the temptation to merge our life with the life of the majority. Separateness involves self-sacrifice; the continuance of our brotherhood is not possible without it. The pain of this sacrifice disappears when the privilege of service is recognised.

CHAPTER III

IN the two previous chapters we have discussed some of the vital principles of Judaism. If the principles are vital, then they must belong to all time. If devotion to the faith made Moses lead a good life in the wilderness thousands of years ago, this same devotion must also help us in England to-day. Life is certainly changed: our work and responsibilities are different, our pleasures and pains are different, our hopes and aims are no longer the same. But, nevertheless, truth *is* eternal, and we are convinced that allegiance to Judaism can make modern life beautiful and good. Indeed, if we are to preserve Judaism as a definite religion, we must show forth its beauty in our lives. Let us by a few examples see how the principles of Judaism can affect and ennoble the conduct of the ordinary everyday life with which we are familiar.

We believe God to be One. Therefore, He is Omnipresent. There is then surrounding us, near us, *in our hearts*, a Being perfectly true, beautiful and good. We know this Being to be God. We cannot see Him; we can only see evidences of His presence when we ourselves are in certain receptive moods. But He is ever present, ever the same. We have by personal experience discovered that He possesses the attributes of love and mercy. But we do not know what He is. When we were children we made fancy pictures of Him as a strong and kind and tender man. But as "grown-ups" we have learnt that He is not Man. Inevitably we think of God as a very fine ether or air all-pervading and penetrating, and we have a little bit of this ether inside us, in our souls, which we also regard as a little something inside our bodies. But this conception is not satisfactory. It is difficult to pray to "air" or "ether." We must try to think of God as a living spirit incalculably more noble and pure than any form of life with which we are familiar. He is spirit, but we know not what "spirit" means. Seeing that He has no bodily form, He has none of the limitations which belong to human life. Possibly He has many attributes of which as human beings we have no conception. The cleverest and best people cannot tell us what God is. They advise us to do reverence to a mystery which we cannot understand, and to thank God for the faith which gives joyousness to our lives and which could not exist without the mystery. This faith is the direct gift of God, and it satisfies a want in our lives by inducing us to pray. If we admit that we cannot understand what God is because He is perfect, and we cannot understand perfection, we shall still be able to realise His presence. We feel a living something within us which is good and makes for goodness if we allow it to control our lives. This something can commune with a Power outside itself. We know by personal experience that this communion is possible and no other evidence of the existence of God is necessary. At any time and in any place we can speak our hearts to God. Therefore we believe Him to be Omnipresent. By communion with God we discover some of His attributes. Because we find God perfectly loving, and merciful and true, we prove by experience the truth of the faith which He has given us. When we pray we experience His help. Through communion with God, our eyes are opened to see the perfectly beautiful elements in His work outside our own lives, and these elements are evidences of His being. They cannot be created by man. They belong to God and reveal His purity. We cannot measure the degree of God's holiness, but we can believe it to be immeasurable. We can derive ever new sustenance from the source of life and believe that the supply can never be exhausted. It is best for us to think of God's *attributes* and not endeavour to penetrate further into the mystery of His being. Enough for us to believe that He works in righteousness. Let us imitate the Psalmist's example and say,-

> "Lord, my heart is not haughty nor mine eyes lofty,
> Neither do I exercise myself in great matters
> Or in things too wonderful for me.
> Surely I have stilled and quieted my soul;
> Like a weaned child with his mother
> My soul is with me like a weaned child.
> O Israel, hope in the Lord
> From this time forth and for evermore."

What difference does the presence of God–with Whom we can have communion–make to us? It makes us care for the right things; it gives us a standard with which to compare our human conceptions; it gives us an ideal. Let us again illustrate our meaning from our conception of love—the best conception we know in life. The existence of perfection outside us, makes us seek the *best* form of love. In marriage it helps us to distinguish between animal passion and spiritual affinity. We seek to make our home life pure and beautiful, free from jarring strife and vicious habits, so that it may be in harmony with the nature of God. God has made us in His image. At the moment of temptation or of anger, we may be saved, if we remember the ideal towards which we strive, and endeavour to let perfect love, existing without, be reflected in our hearts. We cling to this ideal of love, and control ourselves to resist the momentary self-indulgence, which may drive it from our homes. We are ready to make many sacrifices in order to preserve it. The ideal of perfect truth, as well as the ideal of love, may help us in our difficulties. We know how easy it is to lie. Were it not for our belief in the Ideal, we should be sometimes tempted to think that truthfulness was not a really necessary virtue. It seems occasionally so useful to deceive, it helps us to get on. Sometimes our country's laws are irksome and prevent us from doing what we like. For example, the housing laws prevent us from getting the rooms we wish; the education laws force us to send our children to school when they would be useful at home; industrial laws forbid us to employ people under the improper conditions which suit our pockets; anti-gambling laws prevent us from making money in ways convenient to ourselves. Most of these laws can be evaded by skilful deceit. But fortunately such deceit is impossible to people, who realise their responsibilities, when they dare to call themselves Jews. There is a God of truth, and we declare ourselves His servants. We can only serve Him by truth, for no other form of service is acceptable to Him. However difficult the struggle, however unpleasant, we *must* seek to approach nearer to the Ideal of Truth which surrounds our lives. It is near us in our homes and in our workshops. If we want to make our lives at one with God, they must be free from deceit, which is hateful unto Him.

There is another way in which the idea of God's presence can help to raise the standard of our lives. We all know how we feel when we meet a person whom we love and respect very much. We want to be at our best. If ugly thoughts come into our minds we chase them away; we try to do and say the things which would please him. We try to let nothing jar on his standard of good. Now, does it not seem clear that, if in our own lives we could realise at all times God's presence, we should try as hard as possible to be better? The ideal of perfection would induce us to make efforts ourselves to approach nearer to God. We should try to conquer the habits which separate us from Him. Let us just fancy what would happen if one morning all men were to realise the idea of God's presence and cling to it throughout the day. In London the working men and women rushing along in tubes, trains and buses, the women going about their household avocations, the children in the schools, the business men in their offices, the professional men at their desks, the idlers, the workers, rich and poor, learned and unlearned, all these knowing themselves in the presence of God would seek good and not evil. Thoughts, words and deeds would be sanctified; God's rule would be recognised on earth; His creatures would praise Him in righteousness.

The idea of God's omnipresence increases our reverence for life. Life must be beautiful, since God is revealed in life. When we find good people we must respect them, whatever their race or creed or social position. *Their* goodness reflects *God's* goodness. We pay it the homage which is its due. Moreover, no man can be entirely bad, since all men are the children of God. It should then be our effort to discover the influence of the divine, even in characters otherwise brutal. In beautiful works of art, too, we can find God. Sometimes these works of art do not appeal to us at first. Perhaps we have not studied enough to understand them; it takes time to recognise their power and we are too busy to devote this time. Yet when we are told that these artistic creations are the efforts of men and women, who saw God's beauty in the world and tried to reproduce it in their work, whether in music, painting or books, we feel reverence for the artist. We even make an effort to understand his work.

The presence of God is perhaps still better realised, when we are fortunate enough to go into the country, and see God's beauty revealed in nature. When, for example, we lie on the top of a hill covered with heather—lovely in colour and in scent—and we look up to a sky which is perfect in its cloudless beauty, pure joy enters into our soul. The world seems absolutely—God's presence pervades all, and every flower and blade of grass seems to rejoice in His glory.

There is a tendency in modern times to dwell on the ugly and evil side of life. This attitude of mind sometimes leads to coarseness. We revel in things brutal, until we ourselves become less delicate in our sensibility. Perhaps we think that ugly sights and sounds and thoughts cannot harm us, since we can distinguish between good and evil. "Knowledge is good," we say. "Why should we fear it?" This kind of argument often leads young men and women to dull their senses with the study of impurities, and in spite of their self-reliance, they gradually find it more and more difficult to "wash themselves and make themselves clean." Life is short, and while we busy ourselves with the contemplation of vice, the years slip past. Then we have no time to see the glory of the Lord, of which the whole earth is full. We do not seek to approach the Perfect Love and Truth and Beauty which is by our side. We are too busy peering into the mud which lies beneath us.[3]

According to the *second* vital principle of Judaism, the God of the Universe has relations with each individual soul. This belief must certainly increase our self-respect. God dwells, we may venture to say, within us. He blesses our lives with a Spirit emanating from Himself. He requires us to keep that spirit pure and strong with an increasing strength. The body, which conceals, and at the same time reveals that spirit, must be kept healthy and clean. Any impure act, or word, or thought renders us less conscious of the God within us. God has endowed us with the gifts of body, mind and heart, and since we are responsible to Him for our lives, we are responsible for the manner in which we use His gifts. We cannot excuse ourselves by crying that life is short, goodness is difficult. We eat and sleep, work and play, love and die, but is that the end of all? God has given us Eternity in which to complete our lives. He has enriched us with aims and longings which we cannot satisfy on earth. He has bidden us cultivate a learning spirit, and approach with humility and hope the kingdom of the Unknowable.

God has relations with each human soul. He *cares* about each of us, even the smallest and humblest of us. He will help us in our hour of difficulty; if we will seek His help, He will strengthen us. Our joy is pleasing unto Him. He pities us in our times of sorrow. He is ever ready to help us. We need have no fear. "Seek the Lord at all times, call upon Him while He is near." Some of us are apt to think that our lives are of little consequence. It cannot matter much, what we do. In the industrial world, we are not much regarded. We do our work and receive our wages. If we fail to satisfy our employer, he will send us away, and a hundred other people will be ready to take our place. We are *cheap*

---

[3] The problem of the existence of evil is referred to on page 6.

articles. Why should we trouble? Judaism teaches that no soul is cheap. It has dignity, for it emanates from God—its destiny is with God. He cares what becomes of us. He expects us to be good. He will help us to do what is right. If we do our work for the sake of our wages—just well enough to be paid—we are working in the spirit of slaves. We are obeying the law of force. If, instead, we put our best into our work, and do it as well as we possibly can, we are serving God as free men and women should, and our work is pleasing in His sight. We are obeying the law of Love. God loves us. He accepts our efforts to do right, even as in ancient days, He accepted the sacrifices of our fathers which were made in the Spirit of devotion. We need never be afraid to acknowledge ourselves the children and servants of God, "Who brings every work into judgment, whether it be good or whether it be evil." We may venture to ask God to bless our work, in spite of its many imperfections, if we try strenuously to labour in His name.

Judaism teaches[4] that we are directly responsible to God for our lives, that if we sin, we must bear the consequences of our sin. We know that, however much we try, our weakness is so great that our lives must necessarily be imperfect. We can only rely upon God's mercy and love and pity. We must live so that at the end of our lives we may say, as we commit our spirits to God, "We tried to do our best; we remembered Thy trust." It will surely not be enough for us to say, "We never meant to do any harm. We lived from day to day and did our work, and enjoyed ourselves and interfered with nobody." We are put into the world for some higher purpose than to "do no harm." We have to try to do a little good, and to leave a small corner of the world rather better than we found it. There is a meaning and a purpose in our life, since we serve God through our actions. We can never *fully* develop our powers, for they reach towards perfection, and we can never be perfect on earth. We can never do enough in the service of man, for God requires that we should love our neighbours as ourselves, and we can never do enough for ourselves.

The individual life, then, is important because it comes from God and must be re turned to Him, because God loves all His creatures and gives them their strength. Further, no human being can live alone. Each *affects* his surroundings. If his life is impure, he injures those, with whom he comes in

---

[4] *See* page 6, concerning the third vital principle of Judaism.

contact; he sullies God's world; he increases the amount of evil and ugliness which help to conceal the vision of Perfection from those who need it most. Therefore, the love of our neighbours is a necessary development of the love of God.[5] We must labour to give our fellow-citizens the opportunities for self-realisation which we ourselves desire. The progress of the State depends on the progress of the individuals who make up the State. No failure on the part of our neighbours can leave us untouched. If we dare to ignore the need of any human being, on the ground that we are not related to him, we do so at our peril. The God who has fashioned all races of men has bound them together in their dependence on Him. If our duties towards the State are religious in character, the conduct of our home life should surely also be consecrated to God. God sanctifies the bonds which unite husbands to wives and parents to children. In this sense we may believe that marriages are made in heaven. Men and women, who disregard their obligations to one another, forget their responsibilities to the Omnipresent God. When we hear to-day of Jewish husbands deserting their wives, of wives neglecting their duties, we wonder whether our community is going to lose one of its chief glories. In the past, the sanctity of home life was zealously cherished among all sections of Jews. *Mezuzoth*[6] on the doorposts symbolised a truth which was recognised and obeyed. The *Mezuzoth* are now not always discarded from homes where unfaithfulness has banished love. What a mockery ceremonial observance becomes, when it is disassociated from a moral life! We inevitably degrade our inheritance, when we are faithful to ceremonials and forget the ethical teaching of our faith. A man cannot be a good Jew, if he neglects the duties which he has taken upon himself as husband and father. To his children the inheritance of Judaism passes.

We dare not neglect the principles which should inspire our lives and be transmitted to our children. We are charged by God to speak unto the

---

[5] *See* page 7, par. IV.

[6] The Mezuzah is a piece of parchment on which are inscribed the verses in Deut. vi. 4-9 and xi. 13-20. The parchment is rolled together, put into a small case, and fixed on the right-hand doorpost. A small opening is left in the case, through which the Hebrew word for Almighty, written on the back of the scroll, is visible.

generations of His love and of His goodness. If we are silent we sin against God.

As individuals, if not as parents, we must endeavour to render our lives acceptable to God. We have to remember that we are members of a brotherhood that exists for a definite religious purpose.[7] If we bring shame on ourselves, we bring shame on our community. A Jew, who is dishonest in commerce, who engages in degrading pursuits, injures not only himself and his family but also his community. By greed and ostentation we betray our co-religionists, we cause our enemies to rejoice in our discomfiture. Even as our mission is noble, so ought our conduct to be beyond reproach. Judaism cannot influence the world, unless its followers earn the world's respect by reason of their virtue. Not by riches, nor by knowledge, can we cause God's name to be glorified, but by "doing justice, loving mercy, and walking humbly with our God." The charge, which God has laid upon our brotherhood, is a heavy charge. We cannot escape our responsibilities. We would fit ourselves more earnestly their faithful discharge.

---

[7] *See* page 7, par. V.

CHAPTER IV

WE have in the previous chapters enumerated the vital principles of Judaism, and discussed their influence on modern life. We have now to ask ourselves—On what authority do we base our belief? Where do we find these principles established which we have ventured to formulate?

The so-called orthodox section of Jews would reply that these principles do not comprehend Judaism. To them, Judaism means the observance of the Pentateuchal and Rabbinical law, and through obedience to that law they attain to righteousness. The formulating of principles is to them a matter of secondary importance. The supreme duty is to obey the law, which has been handed down from generation to generation, and this obedience teaches them self-restraint and self-sacrifice. This book is not addressed to men and women belonging to this school of thought. To those who accept the verbal inspiration of the Bible and its miraculous divine revelation, religious duty is too clear to require comment. No consideration of ease, self-advancement or parental indulgence can justify the law-breaker, who regards the law, as the embodiment of God's eternal word.

We can feel little sympathy with those, who shirk a duty on the grounds of its irksomeness, who are sceptical merely through selfishness.

These Apostates perhaps deserve some of the anathemas, which are flung indiscriminately at the unobservant—although conversion to religious observance is seldom accomplished by abuse. But in our community to-day, there is a large class of Jews who are unobservant, because their Judaism no longer rests on the authority of the Pentateuch. *They find it instead in human conscience*, in experience and in history.

We have only to formulate this changed conception, in order to recognise its difficulties and dangers. Indeed at the first shock we fancy that a religion based on human conscience, must be a religion of conflicting, chaotic principles. It is only after careful consideration that we are led to a different conclusion, and to realise that a religion based on the authority of conscience, makes a supreme demand on the noblest faculties with which man is endowed. The experience of prayer shews that there *is* communion between man and God, and therefore in the language of our childhood, we may still venture to define conscience as the Voice of God within man, and we need not be afraid to be guided by its authority. It leads us to recognise the existence of the Good, the True and the Beautiful as revealed in all forms of spiritual life, and to find the noblest ethical lessons in the Bible, and in the lives and works of the best men of all ages. Seeing that God is true, we admit that He can only be served by truth, and therefore we are induced to make the conduct of our lives conformable to the highest conceptions of truth, to which, with the help of the thinkers and teachers of all ages, we are able to attain. The best minds devoted to the study of religious history and of the Bible guide us in our search after truth. We dare not be afraid of their conclusions. Judaism must be able to survive the scrutiny of the keenest human intellect, directed towards the sacred literature. It is a sort of blasphemy to withhold mind from the study of God's word.

Earnest, reverent study induces us to believe only in the partial inspiration of the Bible, and in the diverse ethical value of its component parts. We find in the Bible the noblest conception of God and goodness ever given to the world. The Book contains the finest ideals of conduct ever formulated by men, and we dare not disregard its teaching. We dare not neglect the noble, ethical precepts contained in the Bible, on the ground that they are sometimes followed by contributions from less-inspired souls. Let us seek the *best* in the Bible and when we find it, let us admit that God—the Perfect God—has allowed His spirit to rest upon His servants and they have spoken His will. Then let us do homage to their teaching.

There is a terrible danger in evading the duty of seeking God's Word in the Bible. Of course we *can* excuse ourselves in numbers of ways. We can even pretend that we are not certain enough of selecting wisely; therefore we will escape altogether the duty of selection. Let us remind ourselves again, that we are responsible to God for the use of our powers. The consciousness of our imperfections, is no justification for those of us, who are backward in God's service. Moses was slow of speech, but God chose him as His messenger. He gave him the help he needed to do the work which was demanded of him. We need not then be discouraged by the knowledge, that our best intellectual efforts must necessarily be terribly imperfect. We will grope after truth although our sight is dim; our own faults often shut the light from us, *but* God is merciful. When we seek His word with reverence, zeal and humility, God in His unspeakable love allows a ray of light to fall over our lives and to guide our conduct. No single human being can expect during his short life on earth to learn everything about goodness and God. His own limitations and imperfections limit the possible rewards of his search. His want of success convinces him of the existence of heaven. May we not believe that to the gathering of all God's servants from all ages, countries and creeds beyond the veil, there will be revealed complete truth?

We have tried to show in the previous chapters that, without reference to the Bible, man may, by communion, derive from God the principles which should guide a Jewish life, and that by experience he may prove their truth. If thoroughly realised, they stimulate righteous conduct in all who proclaim allegiance to them. But we are a religious brotherhood, and devotion to the Bible is necessary, if we are to perform our mission to humanity. We are guardians of the spiritual treasure which the world has received; we are the descendants of those who bore testimony to the unity of God. Our existence by that unbroken descent is part of that testimony. The record of lives illuminated by the principles of Judaism, is needed by humanity. The gradual development of these principles by Jewish teachers, prophets and seers, helps men of all creeds *to-day* to seek God and to serve Him in righteousness. We are the guardians of these records. Moreover, we need the Bible teaching for ourselves, for it affords us instruction, refreshment, consolation and encouragement. After communion with God in worship, our conscience testifies to the truth of the noblest revelations contained in the Bible. The study of the Bible requires from us self-sacrifice and perseverance. If we would really receive its inspiration, we must seek it in a humble, reverent, learning spirit; we must be willing to *think*, before we hope to understand. If we would sift the best from the less good, we must attune ourselves to the right mood for study. We are not always in the mood for Bible study, any more than we are at all times fit to hear beautiful music or to read exquisite poetry. But it is good to train ourselves to study the Bible for a few quiet moments every day. Thus we may not only become so familiar with its beautiful teaching, that it may gradually affect our minds and characters, but the habit of study may also imbue us with the spirit of reverence.

Through trying to know God through the Bible, we may gradually learn to seek Him in all things good and beautiful.

The Bible narrative records the lives of men and women whose weaknesses and virtues were very much like our own. They felt their dependence on God—that dependence which we all experience. The Psalms also contain the reflections of almost every human mood. In these poems of sadness and of joy, of repentance and of anger, of trustfulness and thanksgiving, there is always the same note of yearning. While speaking their simple word to God—the psalmists yearn to be at one with Him, to let His love enter their souls. As we read of the submission of the human will to the will of God, we begin to understand and to share the longings of a broken and a contrite heart we realise the possibilities of worship and of the union of human beings in the service of God. Some of the Psalms reflect a higher religious tone than others. Even in the same psalm, we often find verses of different ethical value–the products of several grades of civilisation. But we are conscious that no single psalm is insincere. Every word rings true. We reverence it as the expression of a man's soul. Face to face with God, the Psalmist is conscious of his sins; he strains towards perfection and the ideal seems to move higher and higher above his plane, as he struggles upward. As we read, we hear in reply to the Psalmist's passionate cry of disappointment and despair, the whisper of God's love—the whisper which is caught up by the ages and echoed and re-echoed in triumphant sounds of hopefulness and trust. The perfect communion between man and God described in the Psalms gives us courage. We too will say our word—we too will cry to God—we too will shout for joy, since we are alive and have the power to learn and to love. God hears us. God answers us.

For us in these days of moral laxity, self-indulgence and materialism, the writings of the Prophets are full of rousing exhortation. These old teachers are stern in their simplicity. They insist on unselfishness and uprightness, on *effort*. It is no use, they tell us, for us to fill our temples with images of self, and say we cannot see God. God is here in our lives, crying to us to make ourselves clean, to turn to Him and to live.

These prophets made sacrifices for the sake of truth. Again and again God forced His revelation upon them, His truth entered their hearts; they dared not be silent. Sometimes they had to give up their comfort and ease and throw themselves completely into the struggle against evil. Frequently they had to incur the anger of their contemporaries. In the cause of truth they had to speak the word which was nighest to them. They could not flee from God's presence—they could not renounce the charge which He placed upon them.

As we read of these strong men of old we pray God to give courage to our generation. The old struggle is still raging around us, the struggle against religious indifference and negation, against moral weakness and deceit. The sadness of isolation is on God's people; His voice cries and is not heard by men.

The Bible tells us how Jonah was loth to warn the people of Nineveh of the punishment that was overtaking them. They did not belong to his school of religious thought, and he was therefore indifferent to their doom. But the unwilling servant was shewn his error and was made to recognise the universal fatherhood of God. His words of warning caused the people to repent, and, before his wondering eyes, God's mercy was revealed.

A modern *Jonah* would also be forced to warn men of the misery of sin, and draw them by words of love and sympathy to experience the joys of divine communion. We cannot imagine that he would be allowed to leave many members of his brotherhood in indifference or apathy, because they could not, or would not believe in and follow all the words of the law. He would have, nevertheless, to admit that they too were precious in the eyes of the Lord and might deserve to share the joys of religion.

God knows the hearts of men and will surely not judge those as wicked, who endeavour to live honestly according to the light which He has given them.

A modern Jeremiah could not plead pressure of duties, and the pleasures of home life as an excuse for silence, when his eyes were opened to see the materialistic tendencies of his age. The thought of God's righteousness would overwhelm him. He would risk the pain of misunderstanding and invectives. If necessary, he would sacrifice all the joys that sweeten life and go forth among his brethren and force them to come into the light of truth. If he feared the disintegration of his community, the degradation of their faith, he would not cry "Peace! peace!" for to him there would be no peace.

Throughout the Bible, we find the highest precepts for our guidance in every relation of life. We also find many ceremonial ordinances, which we are unwise to disregard. Observances are needed by us as aids to holiness, as reminders of God's goodness. They serve as the best possible links for binding our religious brotherhood together, and as the most helpful of all educational instruments.

We need hardly remind ourselves that the ideal Jewish life consciously led, in the presence of God is a high ideal, too difficult for most of us to attain. To whatever section of the community we belong, we would assuredly make use of all the aids to righteousness which we can find in our Bible. Conduct can never be a matter of indifference to the believing Jew, and he can never be satisfied that his conduct has attained the highest plane of rectitude, for the Ideal of Perfection inspires his life. Observances are necessary to emphasise the bond which unites us with God. Otherwise, with our limited powers of vision, we may so easily become chained to the actual interests of the moment and forget the "Better beyond," which just touches our horizon, and lights it with a beautiful pure light. While seeking an ethical meaning in all our observances, we should remember that the usefulness of ceremonials is immeasurably increased by the devotion of our fathers. The impress of their sacrifice makes these observances more lovable in our eyes. But they have no ethical value, when regarded merely as survivals of an age that has entirely passed away; if they are worth preserving, they must make a direct appeal to the conduct of life with which we are familiar. They should remind us of God's presence and lead us nearer to His throne; they should give the necessary discipline to those who exercise themselves in works of holiness.

CHAPTER V

Religious Observances are Needed as Aids to Holiness

EVEN in the simplest period of human existence, men and women could never have found it *easy* to lead righteous lives. But to-day, when there is so much to do, that we must all necessarily be in a hurry, there seems less time than formerly to think about God and about goodness. Life has become very complicated now that we no longer live huddled together in a ghetto, allowed only to follow certain trades and professions, and obliged to wear badges to distinguish us from our emancipated fellow-citizens.

In England, to-day, every variety of occupation is open to us, and we need guidance in selection. Honest work, well accomplished, is a form of service which we may offer to God for acceptance. It is therefore of supreme importance that we choose our work wisely. The Jew, who recognises the omnipresence of God must lead a consecrated life. He can hardly expect the divine blessing to rest on him, if he spends his time in acquiring wealth by unfair methods. In our seasons of prayer, we seek God's judgment on our work and in the light of His perfection we realise our many failures and ask for help that we may in future act more worthily. Further, the craving for wealth may overwhelm us and spoil our lives by absorbing them, if we do not set days apart for the study of God's laws. Of course, we all know that any day is God's day, that He is ready at all times to hear our prayers, but the interests of the world are often so powerful as to crush out from our minds the memory of His "very present help." By religious observance, we are reminded of God's presence—of the possibility of drawing a little nearer to the ideal of Truth, Beauty and Goodness which surrounds our lives.

We are well provided with pleasures of all sorts in modern England. But these pleasures cease to make life delightful when they are used not to sweeten labour, but as ends and objects in themselves. Moreover, some of these so-called pleasures are degrading, for they can only be enjoyed by those whose self-respect is dead. God means His servants to be happy, to rejoice in His presence. Judaism is altogether misconceived by those who imagine its influence depressing and gloomy. We serve God when we seek pure joy. But it is during our religious observances, that we have time to question ourselves as to our choice of amusements. Are they innocent? we ask. Do they afford us *true recreation?* In the rush and whirl of life, we are inclined to deceive ourselves, and unless we pause every now and then to consider the tendency and motives of our conduct, we may rush into amusements which we can only value as an excuse for vicious self-indulgence. We must hallow the joys of living, of learning, and of doing, by using them in the service of God. Our bodies and minds need occasional refreshment, and we rejoice that the English national conscience is beginning to recognise and to provide for this need. When in our hours of prayer we seek communion with God, we realise that our capacity for pure happiness must be used in the search after the best in life, and the very fact that this capacity can never be completely satisfied, stimulates our faith in immortality.

Religious observances help us to be at peace in the midst of the anxiety of everyday life. We clear a space in our hearts for the love of God to rest there, and in trying to cherish this love, we are able to resist the temptations to greed and self-indulgence, which may assail us.

We cannot fail to be affected by the religious doubts and controversies which rage on all sides of us. In our own souls, we experience our periods of conflict when we question the meaning of the struggle against evil which flourishes in spite of all human effort. We, too, ask ourselves sometimes, "Where is thy God?" Our observances carry us back to the days of our childhood, when with joy in our hearts we went into the courts of God and praised His name. Once more, something of the child trust steals into our hearts and we are satisfied to rest in God and to do His will.

The trust of thinking men and women is different from that of children. It is strengthened by the doubts which have been overcome, and the sacrifices which have been made for its sake. Nevertheless, the consolations of faith are most easily experienced, when we adopt the receptive attitude of children, when we recognise how little we know, and how much we want to know, how small we are, and what great things we should like to do. These moods come most easily to those who are trained in the habit of observance.

There is no pain more troublesome than the pain of monotony, when day follows day with dreary sameness, when we know our work so well that it makes no demand on our imaginations.

It is our observances which help to bring variety into our lives. They suggest possibilities of self-development and of service. They give us time to *think*, and to plan, and to hope. Realities alone can oppress us; in the kingdom of fancy there is joy.

Religious observances strengthen the bonds uniting the members of our brotherhood. When we remember that on certain days, at certain times, Jews all over the world are engaged in the same religious exercise, we feel the stimulus of the corporate ideal. We become more conscious of the mission to which it is our privilege to be called. We read in the Book of Kings how Elijah, after his great triumph over the prophets of Baal, felt overwhelmed by a feeling of loneliness. He had proved himself a faithful servant of God, he had caused his Master's dominion to be acknowledged by those who hitherto had been led astray by false teaching; yet, as he wandered through the wilderness and sank down under a tree to rest, he cried, "It is enough; now, O Lord, take away my life, for I am not better than my fathers." But God bade him arise and gave him more work to do, and reminded him that there were many other men in Israel who, like himself, had not bowed their knees to false gods. For us, too, in our humble lives it is an immense comfort, either in our times of joy or of sadness, to know that we are not alone. Other men are experiencing the same hopes and fears as ourselves; others are seeking to speak their word to God. The feeling of sympathy which binds us as a religious brotherhood is emphasised, when we come together for religious observance.

Prayer is an effort to reach to a higher idea of life; as we strain upwards, we are sustained by the thought that a common purpose inspires us and our fellow-worshippers. On holy days, when we engage in public worship, we become conscious of a desire to serve our brotherhood. Our hearts are kindled on the altars of God, and we become "unashamed of love." No conventionality or artificial distinction can separate us from our brethren in the hour of prayer. Souls rush together in their effort to praise God, the Father of all.

We can hardly over-estimate the importance of ceremonials as educational instruments. Our children cannot realise abstract ideas. In order that Judaism should have a meaning to them, it must appeal to their imaginations. It must also make a demand upon them. All observances should be connected with prayer in the child's mind–prayer in which he must take part, which he must thoroughly understand. In the daily ordering of our children's lives, we naturally set aside certain times for certain duties, and no other claims are allowed to interfere with the allotment of these hours. For example, the hours of school, and of sleep, and of meals are in a measure sacred for our children. We make many sacrifices in order that they should not be disturbed. Surely we are acting most unwisely if we neglect to set aside some time also for worship and general religious training.

We want our children to grow into good men and women, strong enough to accomplish deeds of virtue. At our peril, we neglect to give them the discipline which will lead them to the realisation of God's presence, for God is the source of the highest virtue. If children once acquire the habit of worship, it is never likely to leave them, even when their lives become full of pressing cares and harassing duties and bewildering ambitions. Indeed, as years pass, they will grow more and more *dependent* on the power of prayer to create joy in their lives and to give them courage to overcome every difficulty and danger, which presents itself. The development of life should include the strengthening of our faith. Conduct, let us remind ourselves, is three-fourths of human life. We want our children's conduct to be influenced by the highest ideals; we want them to walk humbly with their God from their earliest years. If they can once feel the influence of God's love in their lives, they will hate sin, for sin prevents them from realising God.

In order that Judaism should be a living religion to our children, its precepts must be transmitted to them with intelligence and loving care.[8] We can, if we will, create an atmosphere in our homes which shall be conducive to prayer and aspiration. If we venture simply and genuinely to admit our conscious dependence on God for strength and guidance in everyday life, we may in spire all the members of our household with that reverence which alone makes sincere worship possible. If we ourselves perform perfunctorily the religious obligations which we recognise in our home life, their inspiring power will disappear. They will be accomplished as tasks irksome in

---

[8] This passage is taken from a paper on "Home Worship and its Influence on Social Work," read at the Conference of Jewish Women, May 1902.

themselves and unrelated to other phases of our daily lives. ... Children hunger for sympathy, and we cannot secure their love and respect more readily than by convincing them that we, as they, are subject to temptations and determined to overcome them; that we too have knowledge of great weakness in the presence of the difficulties which our lives continually present to us, but that we have supreme faith in God's pity and loving kindness. How can we assure them of these facts more forcibly than by inviting them to pray with us? Family worship should be the most powerful link by which children may be bound to their parents and to one another. ... By asking God in the presence *of our children* to bless the work of our lives, we can testify to our conception of the sacredness of work, as the duty we owe to man in the service of God.

By cherishing a knowledge of Hebrew in our homes, we are encouraging our children to appreciate their religious inheritance, for they can through Hebrew better understand the inward meaning of their sacred literature. Also the knowledge of Hebrew strengthens the bonds which unite English Jews with their co-religionists in all parts of the world. But, while recognising the bond of language as an important factor in the religious development of the Jews, we must remember that a knowledge of Hebrew is not Judaism. It is, of course, very satisfactory when our children are good Hebrew scholars. Their learning is likely to lead them to the most useful of all studies—the study of the Bible. But, unless they have acquired the habit of prayer, unless their conduct reveals a devotion to Jewish principles, they will not be equal to the responsibilities which they have received from God. In our home services, then, we must emphasise above all things the necessity of real intelligent communion with God, and our worship must therefore include some "made-up prayer" spoken in all simplicity, sincerity and reverence in the language most familiar to the worshippers.

We would desire to teach our children to love religious observances and to recognise their relation to modern life. This teaching means sacrifice on the part of the parents themselves. Not only have they to be careful to perform their observances in the spirit of prayer, but they must give up time for patient teaching, for answering questions, for making explanations. Children become indifferent to observances which have no meaning to them. When they are told, in answer to their questions, "Read this," "Be quiet," "Go to synagogue," they lose interest in the apparently meaningless observances, and contempt creeps into their hearts. The "throwing off" later is easy enough. If we let our children adrift in the world without giving them the anchors they need on their passage through life, we incur a terrible responsibility. They will have *us* to thank for their purposeless, indifferent lives, for their weakness in times of temptation, for their degradation. We have received a great religious inheritance, and, unless we pass it on in its beauty, we are untrue to our trust. Indeed, it is right to remind ourselves every now and again of the sacrifices which our fathers made in the cause of religious education. In times of persecution, they suffered poverty and every sort of ignominy, in order that they should hand the lamp of the Lord to us in all its brightness. We have to trim that lamp somewhat in order, that its light should be seen by our generation.

If we refuse to give the lamp this attention—if, instead, we place it in a neglected corner, whence its brightness cannot fall on our lives—our children will live in darkness and see evil all their days.

Some of our religious observances have a historical significance which adds to their beauty, for it emphasises the idea of our religious mission. Moreover, in studying the manner in which our fathers celebrated festivals and holy days, we can draw spiritual lessons for ourselves to-day. For example, in Biblical times, *sacrifices* were the important feature of religious celebrations. It seems strange to us, how in any age men should have imagined the destruction of life to be pleasing unto the God of Love, but, in all our wonder, we must not forget to note the spirit which animated the worshippers of ancient days. They chose their most valued possessions, and they gave them up willingly to the service of God. They felt confident of His presence and of His power to answer their prayers. All their ceremonial rites were accomplished with a reverence and dignity suitable to the occasion. To-day, our forms of service are spiritualised, and therefore more in harmony with the views of our generation. But we cannot improve very much on the spirit of reverence and trust and of sacrifice which inspired our fathers. We may even question whether to-day we are sufficiently eager to give of our best in the service of God; whether, when we enter our synagogues, we are really so conscious of the Divine presence as to speak our prayers in the full intensity of faith; whether we do endeavour to reveal in our ceremonies our highest conception of beauty. In some parts of the world, even to-day, our co-religionists celebrate the holy days with trembling. The sword of persecution is still hanging over them, and they fear lest their large assemblies may rouse the superstitious fury of the ignorant populace among whom they dwell. This fear seems only to strengthen their faithfulness. It affords them new opportunities for self-sacrifice. In England we can assemble, confident that our worship will not be molested by our neighbours. This fact should add a new meaning to our songs of thanksgiving and give a new reason for our faithfulness. Our less fortunate co-religionists must be excused, if occasionally the darkness of their surroundings enters into their souls and shows itself by some form of superstition in their services. Any shortcoming on their part should render our duty more obvious to ourselves. Our worship must reveal the most enlightened thought known to our generation. If it is full of meaning and inspiration for the guidance of conduct, its brightness will not only irradiate our own lives and crown them with the most beautiful possibilities, but will also serve to compensate those who suffer for their faith. A meaningless relic of a past civilisation would hardly be worth the sacrifices made in its name. Our religion belongs not only to the past–it is part of the actual life which we leading to-day, and we believe that there is no finality to its glorious possibilities, which may be realised by the generations who will follow us.

CHAPTER VI

IN a previous chapter it was said that religious observances must be tested by their ethical value. If they suggest no moral lesson applicable to modern life, it is our obvious duty to discard them, for their presence is likely to spoil our vision of God. This duty of selection is incumbent on all those Jews who do not believe in the verbal inspiration of the Bible, and who endeavour to devote their reason to the service of God.

But if we study with reverence the Biblical observances and conscientiously test their ethical value, we shall generally be able to derive from them some teaching applicable to the spiritual needs of modern life. Let us remind ourselves that if these observances *do* satisfy these needs, their age gives them special interest, and should inspire us with peculiar reverence. For long life in itself claims our homage, when it represents the accumulated strength of years.

Thus, when we recall the life of Moses several examples of heroism and self-sacrifice inflame our imagination, but the last incident surpasses all in spiritual grandeur. We see him standing up before the Egyptian king and demanding the deliverance of his people. Through a period of anxiety and disappointment we note how he learns something of God's love and power of forgiveness. Stimulated by this conception, he is able later, in spite of his personal vexation, to pray that his people may be forgiven for their faithlessness and discontent. Finally, we see him on Mount Nebo yielding up his spirit to God in perfect trustfulness. Before his human vision, stretches the Promised Land. To his spirit is revealed the ideal of Perfect Love, and he is at rest. He has done that part of the work to which he had been called. In quiet confidence he leaves to his successor the realisation of his own earthly hopes, having lost none of his interest in his people.

We admire the courage and self-sacrifice of the leader in the presence of the enemy, and still more, perhaps, when he is able to forget the base ingratitude of those whom he has served. But the full measure of our reverence is given to him when, on the eve of his death, he exhorts his people "to be strong and of good courage in obeying the behests of their God." So it is with our ancient observances. The devotion of ages kindles them into life; they yield to us the accumulated strength of the past.

I have spoken in previous chapters of the importance of home services, as an educational influence in the lives of our children. But I am well aware that the tenement dwellings in which so many of our co-religionists live, by their want of space make daily family services almost impossible.[9] There is one phase of family life, however, which in every home can and should be sanctified by prayer. I refer to the Sabbath eve celebrations which should bind families close together in the bond of holy fellowship. This observance has never lost the blessings of peace and hope with which it was endowed by the devotion of our fathers, who found in it the expression of God's promise to all who struggle and suffer in the world. As the children draw round the Sabbath lights and sing hymns of thanksgiving to their God, even the poorest, saddest home is made beautiful. A holy peace rests on each tired worker. They all remember that the God of love understands their need and has pity on them, when they try courageously to bear their burdens. Parents and children become conscious of God's purpose in their lives. They realise their responsibilities to Him, and together they enter His courts and reverently ask Him for strength to work out their lives in His service. The beautiful story of Jacob's dream suggests a Friday night lesson. The tired traveller, conscious of the guilt which is upon him on account of his mean conduct to Isaac, lies down by the roadside with a stone for his pillow. It is only then when he is in trouble, when he is cut off from his family and his friends through his own sin, that the idea of God's nearness is revealed to him for the first time and his religion acquires a meaning, which is to influence his life. "And he dreamed and behold a ladder set on the earth, and the top of it reached to heaven, and behold the angels of God ascending and descending on it." Then he hears the voice of God telling him of the work which he will have to accomplish, in order that through him and his seed all the families of the world shall be blessed. "Then Jacob awaked out of his sleep, and he said, 'Surely God is in this place and I knew it not.'" The same desolate surroundings were visible to Jacob when he awoke as on the previous night, the same hard pillow was under his head, but nevertheless the world had changed for him. It was glorified, for

---

[9] Taken from the paper on "Home Worship."

he had begun to feel God's presence. So he went forth to learn more about goodness and God through hard work and self-sacrifice and the sweet consolations of love. God chose him as His Prince, and he spent his life in trying to realise the full meaning of that lesson, of which the first line was learned when he exclaimed, "Surely God is in this place and I knew it not." God is everywhere, and He loves righteousness. This is the lesson, too, which the Sabbath eve teaches, and thus the Sabbath eve observance may serve as a ladder by which we may reach through prayer from earth to heaven. It reminds us of God's presence and beautifies and ennobles our homes. It fills our minds with visions which strengthen us to go about our work and trust to the help of God. It beautifies the darkest corners of our lives with the light of hope. A little girl once said, "If you *are* naughty all the week, you must at least be good on Friday night." The child did not mean that Friday night's goodness made up for the week's misdoings, but she had been influenced by the spirit of aspiration, which belongs to Friday night, and felt that naughty words and thoughts must not be allowed to spoil its holy beauty.

There are Jews influenced by Oriental conceptions, who still seem to think that Judaism is less concerned with women than with men. But the tendency of the Sabbath eve observance is to broaden our conception of Judaism and its ceremonials. We realise their connection with life and their general usefulness. Upon the mother devolves the duty of lighting the Sabbath light, the symbol of the home, hallowed by service. Upon her virtue and godliness, does the purity of the home ultimately rest.[10]

Life would be indeed *earthy* without its Sabbaths and holy days. They give us the *time* so necessary for the tightening of those links, which bind the soul to the God who gave it. Nobody can desecrate the Sabbath with work without being conscious of a serious loss. Only absolute necessity should drive us to Sabbath work. But if the necessity *is* there, it can give us no excuse to sever ourselves from the community. Rather we must make more strenuous efforts to create opportunities of public worship, since through no fault of our own

---

[10] When we hear that some of our co-religionists spend their Friday nights in going to theatres and music-halls, or parties, or in card-playing, we feel that they are making a terrible mistake—a mistake which may spoil their whole lives and the lives of their children. By choosing the wrong time for their amusements they cut themselves off from the highest influences of Judaism. They are even desecrating the sanctity of their homes.

we may be unable to attend the synagogues at times when the authorised services are being held there. If work is honest and hallowed by the conception of God's omnipresence, it will not need any difficult adjustment of ideas, in order that we may pass from our workshop to the house of prayer.

It is possible that existing synagogue forms of service may fail to appeal to some of us. But this indifference should not be an excuse for us to remain away from public worship altogether. The fact that men and women come together in prayer, in itself gives us some useful food for thought, and as we mingle our word with that of other worshippers, our zeal is strengthened by their fervour. We can only hope to influence the form of service authorised by our ecclesiastical authorities, if we can prove it to be unsatisfying after a long and regular attendance. It is no use our saying that we dislike a particular form, and therefore are indifferent to all Jewish worship. We must *care* sufficiently to realise what we lack, and keep so in touch with our community, that when the opportunity arises we may formulate our needs, and be assured of a sympathetic hearing. It has been said that the Sabbath should be a day of rest and of worship. We need rest for our bodies and *change* for our minds; we need prayer to strengthen us for the labours of the week. If we *must* work, we can and should still pray, but the necessity of work should only be admitted when some real sacrifice has been vainly made to prevent it. The Sabbath, besides being a day of rest and of prayer, should be a joyful day–a day when we can find time to rejoice in the midst of our family and friends and realise the message of kindliness which the Sabbath proclaims. It should be a day of pure recreation, when we can have recourse to all sorts of quiet and refreshing pleasures.

Some of us are inclined to point to very observant Jews, whose religious professions are not in harmony with their daily conduct, and to pretend that their insincerity justifies our complete indifference. But this attitude is clearly illogical. Because some men hide their ugly deeds behind the dazzling light of specious holiness, we need not refuse to seek *true* holiness ourselves. It is wiser to put our own lives right and to recognise our own shortcomings than to worry about the failings of our neighbours.

In the next chapter we will consider the meaning of the Jewish holy days and ask how their observance can stimulate right conduct. The general ethical value of holy days, we have already attempted to establish in discussing the helpfulness of ceremonials.

CHAPTER VII

WE can find in each of the "Five" appointed Holy days a deep, ethical meaning, if we would seek it in a reverent spirit.

The *Passover* commemorates the deliverance of our fathers from slavery in Egypt. Some of the details of this deliverance, as recorded in Exodus, are probably, to a certain extent, legendary. Yet we may rightly believe that the descendants of Jacob were working in ignorance and pain for the Egyptian taskmasters, when they wereled forth to the wilderness where Judaism was founded as a national religion. Through this religion, thus founded, all the nations of the earth were ultimately to be blessed. The hurried departure of the Israelites is symbolised in our eating of unleavened bread on the Festival of Passover; many other incidents of their deliverance are commemorated in the "Seder" service. These concrete and picturesque symbols appeal to our imagination, and their observance greatly interests our children and encourages them to study the history of their race. But we do not "keep" Passover by merely refraining from eating leaven in any form whatever, throughout a week, or in forbidding it to pass the threshold of our homes. We must also try to realise the lessons which Passover suggests, and allow them to influence our conduct. On the Festival of Passover we must not forget to thank God for the privileges of our appointment, as witnesses to His goodness and unity. We are heirs to that inheritance which our fathers founded in the wilderness. But we understand more clearly than they possibly could, that this inheritance is one involving work and self-sacrifice. They were told to obey the precepts of the law, in order that their days might be prolonged in a land of abundance. We have learned that our highest good is to be found in works of righteousness, through which the spirit of God may be revealed to the world. Our religion has passed to a broader and more universal stage.

Through studying the history of the Exodus, we see how the thought of God can refine human life The Jews were persecuted slaves, living merely to escape punishment. Their chief pleasures seem to have been connected with eating, and even when the blessing of liberty was conferred on them, they were willing to sacrifice it if only they could taste again the delicacies of Egypt. This same people were taught to acknowledge the tender care and love of God, and gradually they and their children became susceptible to the higher beauties of life. The gentle consideration revealed in some of the laws recorded in Leviticus testifies to the fact, that the Jews had emerged from barbarism. When they came to be surrounded by savage tribes they remained susceptible to high ideals, and gradually evolved the religion to which we are devoted to-day. This transition from barbarism to civilisation was wrought by the gradual recognition of the Divine Father's omnipresence. To-day some of us lead somewhat sordid lives, caring mainly for good food and smart clothes and getting rich. We have not realised God. If *once* the habit of prayer is introduced into our lives, our coarse pleasures will cease to absorb us and we shall experience higher joys. The festival of Passover should remind us that as a nation was led out of its barbarous ignorance by the knowledge of God, to recognise the highest refinements of life, so may we, by communion with Him, attain the blessings of culture, even though we may be of humble birth and means, and have few opportunities for scholastic learning.

Passover is also the festival of liberty. Again and again throughout the Bible we are told to be considerate to the oppressed, because our fathers were oppressed in the land of Egypt. Their sad experiences should inspire Jews of all times to be on the side of justice and humanity in every struggle. The week of Passover gives us the opportunity for self-examination, and we should ask ourselves particularly whether in the conduct of our own lives, in our workshops and in our homes, we are as kind as possible to those who toil for us. An earnest woman who is devoting her whole life to the cause of industrial freedom, tells how her mother worked in the mines in the days before the passing of factory laws, and bore to the day of her death the mark of the overseer's whip on her shoulder. The pain of that blow has inspired a noble life of unselfishness and devotion to the cause of the oppressed. We Jews are the heirs of pain; across those two thousand years which separate us from the slaves in Egypt the sounds of lamentation echo in our ears and inspire us to feel sympathy for all who suffer the misery of persecution, or even the minor pain of loneliness. Thus the festival of Passover rouses our indignation against Russian or Turkish misrule, and also our sympathy for the little servant girl who drudges in our home, or for the shop assistant who ministers to our needs from behind the counter. And this indignation and sympathy should be genuine and far-reaching. If the opportunity arises for us to relieve the persecuted, we dare not hesitate, lest the suffering of our fathers should testify against us. We must also be careful so to order our lives that no profit or pleasure can come to us at the cost of another human being's pain.[11] "Let, at any-rate, the season of the festival not pass away, without our doing something in it, during the very week while it lasts, to make somebody or other a little happier, and to lessen for a little while, or in a small degree, the load of care or sorrow which so many people around us have quietly and patiently to bear.

"The Passover is therefore a festival of hope and consecration, of thanksgiving and gladness, of freedom and charity. It urges us to look forward and strive to be grateful to God the Giver and the Saviour, to bear in mind the claims upon us of the stranger, the fatherless and the widow. Remember the past and work for the future; hope and help; think and thank; be strong and strengthen; rejoice and make rejoice; these and such as these are the watchwords of the Passover."

The second of the great festivals of rejoicing, the festival of Pentecost (the name of Pentecost means the fiftieth day, from the Greek *Pentikonta*, meaning fifty), is celebrated seven weeks after Passover. Its meaning has changed since Biblical times, when in Palestine it was celebrated as a purely agricultural festival. The Passover ritual observances included the offering of a sheaf of barley. On the feast of Pentecost the Jews were commanded to bring two wave loaves out of their habitations and in holy convocation to give thanks for the harvest blessings. Since early post-Biblical times Pentecost has, however, been mainly regarded as a festival to commemorate the giving of the ten words. But we decorate our synagogues with flowers in order that we may be reminded of the old agricultural meaning. These flowers should quicken us to a sense of gratitude to God for the beauties of nature, which belong to all men alike, both small and great. "The festival [of Pentecost] year by year celebrates the promulgation and excellence of the ten fundamental words of religion and morality. It is the festival, which celebrates the great cardinal dogma of Judaism, namely, the necessary union of religion and morality with each other, that is, that God is forever associated with goodness, and that

---

[11] *Bible for Home Reading,* Vol. I. p. 74.

goodness must forever be associated with God. One God, and He the God of righteousness, that is the keynote of Pentecost. Goodness for ever rooted in God, even as God is goodness. The love of God shown in the love of man, and the love of man based upon, and culminating in the love of God. Again, Pentecost is the festival of the family, for it declares that the basis of social well-being is the honour of parents and the sanctity of the home. Then, too, Pentecost is the festival of law, and law is a great and noble element in human life, which will always play its part and maintain its worth. Lastly, Pentecost is the festival, which, through law, bids us in a sense get beyond law. ...

"The tenth word bids us quench the source of evil which is within, cut down desire and lust at their roots within the soul, and, leaving the negative commands of prohibitory law, we advance to the positive commands of morality and religion—Thou shalt love thy neighbour as thyself, thou shalt love the Lord thy God with all thy soul and with all thy might. Pentecost is therefore a great festival of religion and morality, a day, moreover, be it well remembered, suited for the worship not of one people only, but of anybody of whatever race who chooses to join us in its celebration."[12]

We see how Pentecost, if properly understood, can teach us the ultimate meaning of all religious observance, for it is intended to stimulate our moral ideal. We are reminded of the worthlessness of Judaism, *unless* it includes a high conception of morality. We are not Jews, unless we try consciously and steadfastly to be good, and to consecrate our lives to the Omnipresent God.

It is important that we should not let the festival slip by, without devoting some thought to the study of the Ten Words. Year by year we may, with God's help, see more meaning in these commandments, and thus each Pentecost should mark some little advance in our conception of the purpose of life, and the sanctity of its responsibilities. The first commandment bids us dwell on the oneness of God, on His eternal unvarying goodness and love. The second and third demand complete, single-hearted and reverent service. We ask, whether we ourselves are entirely free from idolatry, whether the cult of riches and honour, does not sometimes replace the true worship of God in our "holy of holies," which only the Father's eye can pierce. Are we careful enough in our speech and in our thoughts not to take the name of the Lord our God in

---

[12] *Bible for Home Reading*, Vol. I. p. 143.

vain? The fourth commandment proclaims, to all time, the value of the Sabbath, as the means of uniting man with God in a holy covenant. The fifth summons us to honour our parents. Surely this exhortation is not superfluous in our day, for is it not to-day that men and women incline so persistently to be over-wise in their own eyes, and to underrate the sacrifices made by their parents in the cause of truth?

The sixth, seventh, eighth and ninth commandments admonish us not to transgress that moral code, upon which civilised society is based. They emphasise the sanctity of human life and honour. The tenth commandment, as we have seen, bids us look within, and destroy the root of moral evil, which is envy and lust.

The festival of Tabernacles is still a festival of nature.[13] "It is the festival of gratitude to God, the Giver of our daily bread. It bids us remember all, that in the last resort, we owe to the soil. Just as the essence of character is goodness, and not wisdom, so the basis of our life is not the work of brain but the work of muscle and hand. Life in cities depends upon life in the fields. It was once said that man made the town but God made the country. The saying is not quite accurate, but there is some truth in it." (In the country the surroundings are more beautiful than in towns; there is more regularity and order. This beauty and this order are revelations of God's oneness. We often see in towns, buildings which are inspired by a high conception of beauty, but these works may be spoiled by the cupidity or meanness of the builder. When men become fully conscious of God's omnipresent love and truth, then will their work reveal Him as beautifully as do the rivers, trees, plains and mountains in His open country.) "Now that we have quite got over the danger of worshipping any part of creation, instead of creation's Creator, we must not run into the opposite extreme of error and forget to remember the divine Creator Himself. We must not empty nature of God because we no longer believe that any part of nature is itself divine. ... More especially for the Jews, who have been so long, and are many of them still, forced to live in cities, and to gain their livelihood by barter, and trade, and commerce, the festival of Tabernacles is not the least important of the three. It should not only awaken in us gratitude to God the Giver, not merely remind us that we owe our daily bread in a

---

[13] The following passage, excepting those portions which are bracketed, is taken almost *verbatim* from the *Bible for Home Reading*.

hundred ways rather to God, than to ourselves, not merely exhort us to the virtues of modest simplicity and cleanly strength, which are associated with the tilling of the soil, but it should induce us to remember that the primal and fundamental daily labour of man is labour in the fields. Agriculture is the first and the greatest of the arts of man. No people is in a healthy state of which a certain proportion is not tillers of the soil." ... (There is a natural tendency for men in every community to follow certain trades and professions. It is well, however, for Jews to beware of this sort of concentration. Their peculiar power of adaptation and their wonderful vitality should encourage them to attempt various forms of useful activity. Agriculture makes considerable demand on men's power of judgment and endurance; it also feeds their love of speculation and excitement. It cannot be altogether ill-adapted to the Jewish character.) "But if there are, at any rate in Western Europe, so few Jews" (to-day) "who are agriculturists, it is the more necessary for us all to learn to love nature, and to teach our children to love nature and to know a little, even if it be only a very little, about her ways and her laws and her creatures. An out-of-door life is a good foundation for goodness and religion. We must learn, if we can, to love nature religiously, looking upon her, as the creation of God, and seeking from, and finding in her all the comfort and the strength which we can."[14] If children grow up "streety," if they feel lonely and miserable in the country, without the noise and excitement of city life, we feel that they have lost something for which no material comfort can compensate them. Parents should not grudge any sacrifice which would enable their children to go into the country during the summer holidays, for children may be induced by the influence of nature's beauties to realise better the existence of God. Adult workers also need the rest and peace of country life some time in the year, in order that their lives may be as complete as possible.

The festivals of Passover, Pentecost and Tabernacles are pre-eminently festivals of rejoicing. We are glad, because of God's goodness. We are conscious of His care and love. Prayers of thankfulness should rise to His throne on these festivals, from every Jewish heart. For past deliverances, for present blessings, and for the power of hope, we should thank God and sing songs of praise to Him.

---

[14] So far the *Bible for Home Reading*.

In addition to the three festivals of rejoicing, the latest code added two others of a totally different kind to the yearly cycle. The New Year, which owes its name to an arrangement of the Calendar, with which we are no longer familiar, is a day of reflection and preparation. Its value as an "aid to holiness" can hardly be over-estimated. As we assemble in prayer on the solemn day, we think over the year which is at an end, and realise its many shortcomings. We examine our hopes and aims, and we decide whether they may be used in God's service, or had better be discarded on the threshold of the New Year. The day of New Year prepares us for the most solemn of all days—the Day of Atonement—and the days which divide these two holy days should be used by us for penitent thought and earnest heart-searchings. In Biblical times, the Day of Atonement was a day of *national* purification, for the sins of individual Jews, whether moral or ceremonial, were felt to degrade the whole nation. Our Fathers therefore endeavoured, by priestly rites, and by symbolic self-purification, to remove the stains from their national shield. The nation, as a nation, must be clean, for it was believed to be God's peculiar treasure. To-day, our Atonement ceremony has a more spiritual and personal meaning for us. Each soul is felt to be responsible to his Creator, and his confessions must be made direct to Him. By prayer and penitence, by kind and charitable resolutions, we seek to feel again at one with God. We realise that the great Day of Atonement cannot help us, unless it follows a succession of daily efforts to reach nearer to God, and unless it gives us a new start on a better life, which we strenuously endeavour to lead. "He who says 'I will sin and the Day of Atonement will bring me pardon,' for him the Day of Atonement will bring no pardon," taught the Rabbis seventeen hundred years ago, and it is well for us to remind ourselves that sin cannot be easily wiped out. Atonement can only be accomplished by those, who, persistently and continuously, strive to seek good and not evil all the days of their lives.

We would not escape the consequences of our sins; we could not, if we would. But we endeavour on this most holy day to understand ourselves, and to recognise our weaknesses. Our strength of character, even as the strength of some great work of mechanism, depends on the strength of our weakest part. As we really are bad-tempered, greedy, licentious, proud, selfish or conceited, so we stand bare before our God. His love and pity keep us from despair. We ask His help in prayer. The Day of Atonement is still to us a Day of Judgment, but it is a day of self-judgment. We dare not be tender to ourselves. We tear open our heart, in order to see its full weakness. We are sorry, terribly sorry for our many faults and imperfections, but we must not stop at futile regrets. So long as we are alive, we shall have the opportunity of being good. Year by year, these opportunities should become more clear to us. On the Day of Atonement, we ask in prayer for courage, and strength to devote our lives to God. As the service draws to a close, we make the solemn declaration of our faith in God. "God, He is one!" we cry with solemn iteration. In this cry, we concentrate all the strength derived from a day of thinking and prayer. Its meaning is impressed upon us, and we go forth from the house of prayer resolved to testify by our conduct, to the truth of our faith.[15]

It has always been the custom to fast on the Day of Atonement. In fasting, we give our interpretation of the Biblical precept, "Ye shall afflict your souls." This custom is valuable, because it concentrates the interest of the day on things spiritual. We are not distracted by the pleasures of the table, from our work of prayer and praise. It should always be remembered, however, that this fasting does not comprehend the full duty, belonging to the Day of Atonement. It is merely a means to the accomplishment of that duty. On this holiest of holy days, we prepare our hearts until they are attuned to deeds of righteousness. Mere ceremonials cannot avail us, as ends in themselves. They can only stimulate us to a higher life. This thought emphasised in the beautiful lesson chosen from the Prophets for the Day of Atonement: "Is not this the fast that I have chosen? to loose the fetters of wickedness, to undo the thongs of the yoke, and to let the oppressed go free, and that ye break every yoke? Is it not to deal thy bread to the hungry, and that thou bring the poor that are cast out to thy house? When thou seest the naked, that thou cover him, and that thou hide not thyself from thine own flesh? Then shall thy light break forth as the morning and thy health shall spring forth speedily, and thy righteousness shall go before thee; the glory of God will be thy reward."

---

[15] In order to preserve the joyousness of the day, our Sabbath ritual contains hardly any reference to sin. Consequently, there may be a danger that the thought of repentance, which is really so closely interwoven with the idea of prayer, should, except on the Day of Atonement, be forgotten in our lives. It is important, therefore, that we should remember the great teaching of *that* Day in our private daily prayers.

All the Jewish holy days begin at sunset, and this fact suggests a beautiful spiritual lesson, for the mystery of birth must always be shrouded in darkness. These festivals are full of life, which it is for us to absorb and make our own. It is right that their beginning should be in darkness. The birth of the soul is also hidden from us.

Besides these five appointed days, to which we have referred, there are other feasts and fasts not ordained in the Pentateuch, but observed by many of our brethren. Want of space prevents me from discussing them in detail. But I cannot pass over the festival of Chanukah, which has its origin in the post-Biblical history of the Maccabees, without paying a tribute to its *religious* value. "The mere national aspect of the matter is very small and trivial; whether a petty tribe of folk called Judæians preserved their separate national existence and constitution, or became assimilated with the Hellenistic Syrian subjects of the motley kingdom of Antiochus was unimportant, when looked at from a merely political or national point of view. But it so happened, that this small race possessed at that time the purest and truest conception of God and of the manner of serving Him among all the races of the earth, and if therefore, this race had then been destroyed or absorbed in the mass of Greeks and Syrians, this religion would also have perished. The work of the Prophets would have been in vain. It would, as it were, have had to be begun all over again. The Maccabæan victories insured the continuance of the teachings and writings of Amos and of the Isaiahs. Therefore, the festival of Chanukah is a *religious* festival, and as such is worthy of our high regard. We are not specially concerned with the defeats of the Syrians. The details of the fightings, subsequent to the dedication of the Temple are of smaller interest to us. The Maccabæan family itself, suffers from the results of conquest and victory. But the preservation of Judaism at a time of imminent and critical danger, remains a permanent fact of supreme importance. If Judæa had been overcome and absorbed, the Jewish congregations outside it, would very probably have been unable to outlive the shock. Therefore we owe our gratitude to the martyrs and soldiers whose festival we celebrate in the days of Chanukah. Let Chanukah be also a festival of courage, a fourth part of all virtue, as the Greeks of old believed. The courage which Judaism demands of us now, is not the courage of soldiers upon the battlefield, but it is often courage none the less. Let the deeds of martyrs and soldiers in the age of Antiochus inspire us from year to year anew."¹⁶ We need this inspiration today, when it requires courage to show allegiance to the teachings of Judaism. Again and again we are tempted to let evil pass, when it seems not to concern us directly, and so we are faithless to our ideal of righteousness. Often Freethinkers seem to be more popular than Jews, and we are sometimes inclined to conceal our faith in order to share their popularity. The Chanukah lessons should make us ashamed of such cowardice. We bow our heads in memory of the heroism of Judas Maccabæus, and pray that it may inspire our lives.

Besides the historical narrative and the precepts concerning ceremonials and festivals, the Pentateuch contains a number of moral laws which deserve our attention. These enactments are mostly concerned with brotherly love and charity. They also formulate a high moral standard in business and home life. Some of these laws can no longer affect our lives, for they refer to conditions which have passed away. In a few instances, the ethical code has been superseded by more enlightened conceptions, and there are many phases of modern life, for which the Pentateuchal laws provide no guidance. These facts should only serve to stimulate our interest in these Biblical books. In the midst of verses, which give no inspiration to modern life, we find passages of inexhaustible spiritual strength. The Pentateuchal laws also include a series of dietary laws, which are valuable, both on sanitary and on ethical grounds. These laws have been observed in post-Biblical days with a remarkable devotion, and even to-day, they are respected in homes in which all other ceremonial laws are broken. To the clear Biblical precepts concerning forbidden food, the Rabbis have added a series of ordinances, which have been accorded almost equal respect. Many of the so-called Mosaic dietary laws are in harmony with modern hygienic principles, and we can only marvel at their antiquity. Moreover, the self-control which their proper observance requires, has been essentially useful to our community, and has trained them in habits of temperance. Unfortunately, the legal minutiæ added by the Rabbis, have here and there somewhat distorted the vision of believers, who have been so misled as to call themselves Jews merely because they kept "Koscher" homes. The effect of such exaggeration, has been disastrous to the spiritual life of our community. It is for us Jews, who aim at making our Judaism a living, ethical

---

¹⁶ *Bible for Home Reading*, Vol. II. p. 740.

influence in our lives, to reveal a sense of proportion in our observance. We must reverently examine these laws, and, where they are in accordance with hygienic truth, and secure the most humane treatment of animals, we should give them our allegiance. In seeking truth, we are testifying to our faith in God. As education improves, we are happily less and less affected by the discipline of our appetites. There are so many pleasures, which appeal to us more strongly than the pleasures of the table; nevertheless, we are not so impervious to temptation, that we can afford to undervalue the lessons in self-control which sound dietary laws enforce. If regarded as a means of purification, they are in harmony with a strenuous religious life, and should therefore be observed in a kingdom of priests.[17] Moreover, in so far as they are consistent with the best scientific principles, known to our generation, they form a valuable part of that inheritance to which we must remain faithful, if through us, the whole family of the "earth is to be blessed." Such fidelity can only strengthen our conception of the innumerable sacrifices, which Judaism demands of us in the cause of truth and righteousness.

---

[17] Compare *Judaism as Creed and Life*, by Mr Morris Joseph, p. 185, par. I:—"These Dietary Laws ... may help to maintain Jewish separateness; they may preserve the idea of Israel's consecration, they may exercise a powerful influence upon personal purity. The last two objects are obviously desirable in themselves. They are more even than this, they are vital objects. The consciousness of being an elect people, and a power of setting an example to the world of personal holiness, are alike essential to the fulfilment of our divinely-appointed errand. Every law that strengthens these qualities, merits respect and obedience. It is a law which still fulfils a great purpose. It is a living law, and therefore a law that deserves to live."

Mr Joseph rests the value of the dietary laws to Judaism, on purely religious grounds.

CHAPTER VIII

I HAVE now given a brief exposition of the fundamental principles of Judaism, and have shown that their realisation, depends primarily on their being applied to the conduct of every-day life. Such application presents, as we have seen, great difficulties to the average man, who needs the help of religious observance and Biblical study, in order that he may understand his responsibilities as a Jew.

Hence the justified appeal to all Jews, to prove their faithfulness to Jewish ideals. Earnestly and prayerfully, we must begin the work of adaptation and reconstruction. The old truths live for ever. They must be rendered comprehensible through their symbols; they must be revealed in daily conduct and in ceremonial observance. The non-religious Jew is a menace to Judaism; his ideals are often a travesty on the ideals of our faith. Yet we should be unfaithful to our mission, if we ignored those, who only claim to be Jews, in so far, as they possess a certain pride of race, but who give no heed to religion. We must not deny them the privileges of our Brotherhood, but we must rather seek to win them to religion, and to a more religious conception of Judaism. As things now are, many of them help to strengthen the materialistic tendencies of our age, against which, we have undertaken to labour.

It is clear that Jews, who live from day to day, indifferent to the claims of religion and moral aspiration, make our brotherhood hateful in the eyes of our neighbours. Generalising from a few instances, of gross materialism, our critics affirm that we are a degenerate people, existing only to advance our own interests. It is for us, who *care* about Judaism to try to show in our own lives its power of inspiration. Thus we may win the most indifferent back to their allegiance, and prove that our religion can satisfy the needs of posterity.

We must try to show the efficacy of prayer and faith in our lives by seeking God's guidance in the ordering of our daily pursuits. If we labour, so that every night we may venture to ask God to bless the work of our hands; if we seek in prayer every morning, strength to accomplish satisfactorily our daily tasks, we shall surely endeavour to work from pure, unsordid motives and to do all we have to do as well as we can. We pride ourselves justly on being a *practical* people, but even practicality can be over developed and so leave too little room for ideals. Some of us are rather ready to denounce our neighbours as mere visionaries, because their lives are uninfluenced by utilitarian instincts. We forget that our history is glorious through the record of lives, devoted to study, and this devotion is a form of idealism.

When their political importance and the outward symbols of their greatness had vanished altogether, our ancestors turned their attention to learning. Their schools were to be the source of their glory. They spent their lives, in attempting to unravel the difficult problems of religion and of life. In the volumes of philosophical and theological literature, which have come down to us, there may be some hair-splitting and confusion of thought. But the spirit of unselfish devotion and of reverence for intellectual work, which animated the writers, is surely not without its inspiration to-day. The men who gave themselves up to study, were heroes in the sight of their contemporaries. They were followed and loved, and their most trivial utterances were recorded by their disciples with absolute fidelity. Even the men, who devoted themselves to transcribing the scrolls of the law, recognised their work as *holy*, and devoted to it a patient courage which is in every sense admirable. We cannot dwell on this page of our history, without being profoundly moved by its pathos. The people had lost their temple, which, in spite of the warnings of their prophets, they had believed indestructible. The interest of their lives had to be now altogether changed, for it had centred round Jerusalem. At the moment of their degradation and misery, God revealed to our ancestors their glorious mission. It was not merely to build and to preserve a magnificent temple, that God had kept them alive, and had led them by the rays of His own light through the darkness of the ages. The Temple was merely the symbol of an eternal truth, and it was as witnesses to this truth, that the brotherhood must exist. Their conduct, their holiness *mattered* to God. Dispersed among all races, despised and even hated by men of other creeds, they were to carry out the glorious charge which had been laid upon them. We can imagine the tremendous uplifting, which such a revelation must have given to people, bowed down by the burden of misery and defeat. Much was expected from them. They were not to waste their time in miserable, useless lamentation. They were to readjust all their ideas and aims, and cease to care about material prosperity, and political glory. As the guardians and depositories of a great religious trust, they learned to rejoice in their responsibilities, and obtained, by intellectual and spiritual striving, a happiness, which was destined to be real and lasting.

We have no space in which to follow the gradual development of the commercial talent of the Jews. That talent received a powerful stimulus under the new conditions of their life in the lands of their dispersion. In addition to learning, commerce began to flourish among them. Indeed, the former depended in a great measure upon the latter, for scholars need bread on which to live, and the results of profound intellectual research, do not always prove of material value. Throughout the dark ages of mediæval superstition, the Jewish traders and scholars were not necessarily two distinct classes, but there were always enough men willing to devote their attention entirely to study. The synagogues worked in connection with schools. Unfortunately, here and there, the thirst for gold got possession of some trader's soul, and he became engrossed in his work, and indifferent to the spiritual claims of his brotherhood. He became, perhaps, rather unscrupulous, when he found honest careers closed to him, and had recourse to question able means of obtaining self-advancement. The light of learning, however, was never quenched among our people. The enthusiasm for God's work flourished among them, as a community, in spite of the frequent lapses of individuals into disgraceful undertakings.

To-day we must remind ourselves, that we are descended from the People of the Book, as well as from those, whose commercial sagacity brought honour to their race. We should recognise that through any honest work, we can testify to our faith in God, and that no shame can attach to careers, which are conducted on honourable lines, for they give opportunity for the realisation of the highest ideals in conduct. In dealing with our fellow-workers, and with the public through our trades or professions, "We can labour with clean hands and a pure heart," and observe Hillel's golden rule, "What is hateful to thee, do not unto thy neighbour." But we must remember the lessons of the past. The thirst for gold does grow with success, and since our people are so clever at getting on, they must beware of the temptations, which are so often connected with material triumphs. In order that our community should be true to its trust, material success must not be its distinguishing glory. Jews must show to the world that material comfort is useful, as a means to an end. People cannot feel the claims of the higher life satisfactorily, while they are hungry and ill-clothed and badly housed. These physical needs *must* absorb their attention. The spirit acts through the body while we are on earth, and it is absurd to ignore the claims of the body. But the joys of study, of complete self-surrender to philanthropic ends, must also not be for gotten by our generation. There are careers open to men and women, which can bring no wealth and very little worldly fame. But they are glorious in the sight of God, and should therefore appeal to those, who are summoned by their faith to minister to Him. There are unpopular causes to be won by our generation. There is work to be under taken, of which the results will belong to posterity. There are trades and professions open to us, which demand perseverance, self-sacrifice and self-denial, and offer no allurement of great personal profit. As Jews, we must remember all these possibilities for self-devotion, and seek to claim some for ourselves and for our children. A father once said of his daughter of six, "I don't want her to go to Sabbath School, I want her to learn how to earn money!" This man was a Jew by race, but he knew nothing of communion with God. He lived in a narrow, cheerless world, guarded by the idols of gold, which be worshipped. He denied to his child the inheritance of Jewish womanhood. She was to be a money-grubber like himself, to find pleasure merely in getting wealth. She was to be shut out from the kingdom of pure joy.

It is by prayer that we learn to sanctify the claims of the body, and make them subservient to a higher life. Morning and evening, we remind ourselves, that there is a God above us, who expects the best from us. Faith teaches us, that we must not live for the pleasures of the hour. "We leave *now* for dogs and apes, we have *for ever*." Therefore we should not be afraid to allow ourselves to be inspired by the lives of our ancestors in the early centuries of the Christian era. We, too, must devote much time to the development of our religious ideal. Indeed, if, as we profess, we really believe that our religion is based on progress, we, as a brotherhood, must endeavour, by strenuous, self-denying effort, to receive some new particle of knowledge from God, and to transmit it to the next generation.

Faith should not only help us in the choice and conduct of our active lives, but should also make us strong in the power of endurance. We remember that

Job, when he was suffering every conceivable misery known to man, when he was bereft of all his children and his possessions, when he was being sorely tried by physical disease, became gradually conscious of the mystery of God's love and the power of faith was kindled within him. He had been rather a self-righteous man, unaware of his own spiritual needs and limitations. God, through His chastening, taught him to realise His presence. The problem of suffering and evil, continues as in the days of Job, and we have to reconcile it with the existence of an Omnipresent and perfect God. Evil exists. Therefore God allows it to exist for He is all-powerful. We cannot solve the mystery of evil. Our faith can only suggest palliatives, which render its existence more endurable. We admit that some evil is the result of wrong-doing. If we indulge in frequent uncontrolled tempers, we gradually alienate our relations and friends if we have recourse to gambling or drinking our moral sense becomes weaker. We neglect our duties, and misery falls on ourselves and our homes. Then again we may commit some deed of treachery or impurity, beyond the reach of civil or criminal law, and conceal it so well, that the world knows nothing of it. Yet this deed will sooner or later make us suffer. We cannot escape its results. "Be sure," says the Bible, "that your sin will find you out." Some people may refuse to be deterred from evil by the fear of punishment, but they cannot be altogether unaffected by the knowledge, that their children will suffer for their sakes. Surely no stronger incentive can induce men and women to lead steady, pure lives, than the knowledge that, if they sin, the consequences of shame and guilt, must be shared by the beings, whom they love most in the world. Punishment which follows sin, is just and comprehensible, even to our limited human understanding. But much evil exists, which is by no means the result of sin.

"Some forms of suffering can be shot through with explanatory and ennobling light, which makes them bearable and even good; but other forms remain dark and inexplicable. The sufferings of sentient animals, and more especially the sufferings inflicted upon them by thoughtless and cruel men, continue to be a hopeless puzzle. Among mankind there are evils such as idiocy, madness and moral degradation which seem beyond explanation. There are problems respecting the relation of civilised to uncivilised races; there are problems respecting the endless individuals, who have lived and died without any approach to that mental and moral stature, of which mankind is capable. There is not merely the strange difference, which oppressed the mind of Job, between the happiness of this man and that; but we ask, and ask in vain, what can be the meaning of that suffering and squalor which do not ennoble or purify, but lead in many cases almost inevitably to sin and depravity? To these, and many similar problems no answer can be given; we, no less than Job, must simply trust in the infinite wisdom and righteousness of God.

"On the other hand, for certain aspects of suffering there are ennobling alleviations."[18]

Were we not acquainted in some measure with pain, misery and sin, we should hardly be able to appreciate goodness, happiness and virtue. We recognise that, as physical life is strengthened by the surmounting of obstacles, so moral life is purified by the struggle against sin.

"We all of us have seen how in times of trial and trouble, people are frequently at their best. Unexpected reserves of goodness and self-sacrifice, are then displayed. The brave endurance of misery at home, the ardent struggle to relieve it abroad, and the good fight against degradation and sin, have provided, and still provide, the noblest opportunities for the exhibition of human patience, pity and human love."[19]

In spite, however, of all these alleviations we must admit that misery and pain are awful while they last. The righteous suffer with the wicked; the helpless and innocent with the guilty. Faith alone can help us to face these facts courageously and patiently. I doubt whether a man who, in the midst of an honourable, independent life is suddenly afflicted with some horrible disease, which renders him for an indefinite period of time a burden to himself, and to his family, can derive much comfort from the hope of compensation in another world. The only real comfort in such cases must lie in the belief that there *is* some explanation for the existence of evil, for God is good. We therefore cling gratefully to our faith in immortality and believe that "beyond the veil," in God's own good time, we shall know, why the hitherto unexplained misery was allowed to exist on earth. Let us then be at peace and trust in God. Evil is no little thing; its presence is hateful to us. God bids us fight against evil and misery with all our strength, but when we can struggle

---

[18] *Liberal Judaism*, p. 66, by Mr C. G. Montefiore (Macmillan).
[19] *Liberal Judaism*, p. 67.

no more, we have the sublime comfort of faith. God knows best, we say, and, through our tears, we look at the world and think it good.

We cannot claim that faith, however deep and sincere, can remove pain altogether. But the recognition of an omnipresent God of love gives us power to bow our heads, and to endure courageously what we cannot overcome. God loves us. So long as we live, He has work for us to do. We must take up our burdens in the spirit of David, who, when, he had vainly endeavoured to save his child, ceased to mourn, and went about the work of his life. We cannot in this world understand the mystery of pain; we must believe in the God of love. He can give us peace. We must seek it from Him. Job was helped by his suffering to realise God. Our periods of suffering also, must be sent to us for our good, although in the moment of agony, we cannot help sometimes wishing that some other method of purification could have been chosen. Gradually, however, in answer to our prayers, the power of submission is vouchsafed to us. Here again, faith is justified by experience. Those of us who have suffered and have prayed, who have put our grief behind us, and let it inspire us to further effort in the cause of God, know that the divine help was not withheld from us. We have issued from the fire, scarred, perhaps, but stronger, nevertheless, in our love and in our faith.

If we can only believe in the vital principle of Judaism, in the omnipresence of a God of love and of righteousness, no incident in life can be intolerable. Every experience must have its meaning and its purpose. When we rejoice, we shall rejoice more completely, if we see God's love and care revealed in that joy. It is not a mere chance, that we are happy. Our happiness is sent to us for a purpose, for we must use it in God's service. When we are sad, God knows about our sorrow and pities us. He will give us peace.

We believe in immortality. We need another life, in order that we should have more time in which to grow good. God is Perfection, and towards Perfection we are bidden to strive. Every sorrow and every joy—everything, indeed, that happens to us in our lives—can be used as a means, by which we may reach higher and higher on the upward road. But we shall not get very far, for we are, even the best of us, very foolish and weak. We must accept that fact at once. "We do not want the future life for punishment, still less do we want it for reward; we do not even so greatly want it for the redress of this life's inequalities in outward prosperity; we do want it for the progress of men towards Perfection."[20] With the hope of immortality in our hearts, let us as Jews live our lives, for how *can* we live as if to-day were the end of everything, seeing that we believe every soul to belong to God and to have emanated from Him? What do the little things matter, the pleasures of gain, the petty cares, the trivial disappointments? Our God knows us from afar. In His love, let us rejoice. Through His light let us see light.

---

[20] *Bible for Home Reading*, Vol. II. p. 207.

CHAPTER IX

SUMMARY AND CONCLUSION

WE have tried in the preceding pages to give our conception of the vital principles of Judaism. We have affirmed our belief that any man or woman may claim to belong to our brotherhood who is convinced that:–

1. There is one sole Creator or God.

2. The God of the world has relations with each individual soul, and each soul, being an emanation from Him, must be, like Him, immortal.

3. We are responsible to God for our conduct, and if we sin, must bear the consequences of our sin. No intercessor is possible or necessary, between man and God. The divine love enters into the hearts of those who seek it with prayer and contrition.

4. The love of our neighbours is a necessary development of the love of God.

5. The Jewish brotherhood exists for a definite religious purpose, and this purpose involves the highest efforts of self-sacrifice and self-realisation.

We have shown how these principles can affect our daily conduct, and how their influence may be strengthened by ceremonial observance and by the study of the Bible. We have emphasised the duty, which is incumbent on all believing Jews, of making the conduct of their lives, in its religious, as well as in its secular phases, consistent with the highest thought known to their generation, and inspired by the dictates of their conscience. In developing these conceptions we have, for the purpose of discussion separated religious duties from secular duties, but we have, nevertheless, emphasised our belief that Judaism affects every relation of life, that it should hallow our conduct on week days as well as on Sabbaths, and holy days. A Jewish life is consecrated to God by the very conditions of its existence. Finally, we made an appeal to our generation to realise themselves, and to become conscious of their own inheritance. Some of the old religious landmarks have been shifted or destroyed by the flux of time. Some ceremonials have lost their significance, and therefore their vitalising power is dead. Superstition has here and there been interwoven with dogma, and the materialistic influences of our age have degraded us. The time has come for us to reconstruct our doctrines on the old foundations of love and trust. We dare not slide along from indifference to negation. A life, unhallowed by religious aspiration is necessarily a sordid life. If we shut out God from our midst, we shall sink into ignorance and extreme degradation. Our children need the faith by which our fathers lived. The continuity of testimony is demanded by humanity. It is part of God's plan to visit the sins of the fathers upon the children unto the third or fourth generation. Do we, in the face of this terrible warning, dare to remain indifferent to the claims of our children? Seeing that God has shown us, through His holy men, that light is given to those who seek it steadfastly and earnestly, we cannot allow our children to live with us in darkness, and pretend to be satisfied and at peace.

The teaching of Judaism inspires us to seek the best in life. We cannot be content with spiritual stagnation. Around us, are many signs of disintegration. Men and women, professing different creeds marry in an irresponsible spirit, and the work of transmission is arrested; men and women, Jews by race, marry, while still unconscious of any living religion whatever. Perhaps their wedding is celebrated in synagogue, but their lives remain unconsecrated to God, and their children grow up indifferent to any claim beyond that of self-advancement. By certain sections of our fellow-countrymen we are unloved. Much of the so-called anti-Semitism is ignorant and unjustifiable. It is rooted in prejudice and in jealousy, but a little of it surely is not undeserved. If men and women live and die as mere earth worms, if they seek to get rich by any means within their power, indifferent to the presence of God, and to the duties of citizenship, anxious merely to enjoy themselves, to eat and drink as much as possible, to wear fine clothes and to look smart—can we wonder that they win the hatred and scorn of the general community? When these same people call themselves Jews—pretending to be members of the brotherhood appointed to testify to the existence of a God of love, truth and beauty—do we not ourselves feel utterly ashamed? God has commanded us to seek Him with love and self-sacrifice, and humility of heart. He has taught us to recognise the vanities of life, by comparing them with His reality. He has bidden us to draw nigh unto Him—to seek peace from his love, to reflect His ineffable beauty in our feeble efforts after righteousness. What are we doing? How are we living? Are we not often false witnesses ourselves? Are we not also responsible for those who take His name in vain by calling on Him with their lips and denying Him in their hearts. We can commune with the living God by prayer. Do we pray? When do we pray? Do we pray at home before work in the morning, and before sleep in the evening? Do we pray in our synagogues? Do we pray to *God*? Do we *think* when we pray? Do we realise God's presence? Do we put our best into our worship? Does it exact self-denying effort from our souls? Is it indeed communion?

Then, again, how about our children? Our fathers gave us bread to eat; this bread will not exactly suit our children's palates. Is it right then that we should give them stones? Can we not make some effort to bake the bread anew and add a few modern ingredients, so as to render it more acceptable to the next generation? If we can do this, our children may live, otherwise they will surely die—the worst of all deaths, for their bodies will live. How shall we account for our negligence to God? How shall we justify ourselves before His throne?

These questions probe us to the depths of our souls. It is good that we should ask them. We cannot live in a fool's paradise, and say all is well. It is not well with our brotherhood. We cannot see the best life among us, joining itself with the life of other communities and say, "Alas! we cannot influence this desertion." We dare not see the worst life slipping into the sloughs of materialism and degradation and say, "What can we do?" and pass on. We ourselves are responsible, for we have not made sufficient effort to make our conduct reveal our faith, to make that faith more real and vital, to test the power of prayer as a living force in our lives. We must rouse ourselves now, immediately. Mere acquiescence is cowardice; it means spiritual death. What can we do?

1. We can try to lead better lives, by realising our responsibility to God and to our brotherhood.
2. We can pray, and allow God's love to affect our lives.
3. We can study the Bible and all the beautiful and pure works of the best men of all ages.

4. We can work among the members of our community, and show them the love of God as revealed in our lives, and by our friendship with them, we can lead them to God.

5. We can examine our religious ceremonials, and faithfully observe all those, which can stimulate righteousness in our lives.

6. We can help to organise, and then take part in the public worship which satisfies our spiritual needs.

7. We can, by example and by precept, by sympathy and exhortation, transmit to our children a living religion, based on a pure conception of the reality of God and His laws of righteousness.

It may be urged that the tendency of lax Jews is to join the larger Christian community, and that the Christian ideal of righteousness is as noble as our own. Why therefore should we strive to prevent defections, which can in no way affect the progress of the human race? The burdens and responsibilities of Jews are so heavy; why should we fret ourselves if some members of our brotherhood choose a lighter religious discipline, in order to arrive at the same end. But we cannot console ourselves so easily. Men and women do not *drift* into the realisation of a new faith. By mere indifference to Judaism, they do not become Christians. By self-denying, strenuous spiritual effort alone, can we realise any religion at all, and certainly no conscientious *change* of faith is possible without it. We know ourselves with what painful anxiety, we, who have been trained in the orthodox school of Jewish thought, pass at the dictates of conscience to liberal Judaism. It seems at first as if our faith must altogether crumble away, when some of our old convictions become in any degree modified. It is a serious and painful duty to refuse homage to observances which certainly jar upon our sense of truth. We do not perform this duty in a careless or irresponsible spirit when these observances are interwoven with some of the happiest memories of our childhood. When we do refuse to stifle our conscientious questionings, and to profess a creed to which we are really indifferent, the change must cause much pain and sorrow to ourselves. For a time, at least, we feel as if we were adrift on the vast sea of scepticism, with no rudder and no anchor. Perhaps we also cause pain to those we love, and would give our lives to please. But the search for truth is God's work, it must be accomplished in the teeth of every conflicting consideration. It is only when we are embarked on this search, when we have rejected that which appears false to our intellectual conceptions, and have refused to conform outwardly, when our spirit is unmoved, it is only then, that we can feel at one with our God. This transition from different schools *within* our brotherhood is then accompanied by sad and difficult experiences. A transition from one creed to another must be infinitely more difficult and painful.

Most Jews who drift from Judaism drift into nothingness, whether their faith has the name of any existing creed, or is too indefinite even to be named. Moreover, just as we cannot become Christians merely by ceasing to be Jews, so we are not Jews merely because we are not Christians. We have to realise our inheritance and let it influence our lives, otherwise only the noblest souls among us can steer clear of materialism. And the materialism of Jews is of the lowest and most gross order, perhaps because the height from which they descended, is so glorious in its possibilities. We can only arrest this descent, by ourselves climbing nearer the heights, and proving by the joyousness of our lives, that we realise the blessings of Judaism. Thus, too, and thus only, can we arrest the departure of those truly religious members of our brotherhood, who leave our community, because its forms and ceremonies offer them so little spiritual satisfaction. We have tried to show in previous chapters that, with a little readjustment, the highest spiritual lessons can be gathered from the ancient observances and practices. We must by our efforts re-trim the lamp of Judaism and cause it to shine with a beautiful, pure light, which cannot be extinguished.

As Jews, we believe our religion to be based on irrefutable principles. Any defection from our community, we regard not only as a loss to ourselves, but as an injury to the proselyte. It is well with us as Jews. We are conscious of the Omnipresence of God. We feel the influence of His love. We obtain strength from our direct communion with Him.

It is our mission to draw men within our brotherhood. We dare not let them pass away, without making an effort to reclaim them. Moreover, at this moment it would seem that our mission is drawing nearer to its accomplishment.

For, passing from other faiths, we believe that men are gradually coming to worship the God of Israel, and to recognise the unity of His being and the law of righteousness, which He has established. Even now we see a gradual approximation of men of all creeds. The Trinitarian idea is accepted with intellectual reservations by believing Christians. The conception of three Entities, seems to be merging into the recognition of different attributes in the one Divine Being.

Christian divines insist more and more on personal responsibility in the conduct of life. The universal Fatherhood is being so much better understood that the doctrine of everlasting punishment for the unbaptised, is being discredited. Then, again, other communities are coming into existence on purpose to minister to the one God, and to worship Him simply and directly by prayer, and by works of righteousness. These new Churches recognise most of our "principles," and we consequently feel in close sympathy with them. All these signs of the times awaken our gratitude and stimulate our trust in the God of truth; they affect our religious obligations by strengthening them, for the faith which inspires us is now being quickened by hope. It sometimes occurs, in the history of scientific discoveries, that two men, working under different conditions, in opposite parts of the globe, alight on the same truth by different methods. The truth of the discovery is not for this reason less valued; rather is it doubly proved. Similarly, our devotion as Jews to Judaism is strengthened, when we find that some of the constituent elements of our faith, are being received more and more favourably by sister religions. The general approximation of different communities can be facilitated in two ways, and both are surely desirable, because universal religious brotherhood will put an end to religious strife, the most bitter of all forms of human strife. In the first place, we can study the doctrines of other faiths with reverence and respect, and we shall find among them some developments of Jewish dogma, which will help us in our search after God. We can gratefully adopt such teaching, as is consistent with the principles of Judaism to which we subscribe. For example, we shall find, in the New Testament,[21] important and suggestive modifications of the doctrines of retribution and of the relations of suffering to sin, a fresh and noble restatement of the old prophetic doctrine, "I desire love and not sacrifice," among doctrines which to the Jewish mind are narrow and harmful, a passionate enthusiasm for the moral and religious regeneration of the outcast and the sinner, fine teaching about the nature and power of love

---

[21] *Bible for Home Reading*, Vol. II. p. 779.

and the duty of forgiveness, fresh contributions to the conception of self-sacrifice, suffering and religious inwardness ... a striking presentment of the true and intimate relation of the human child to the divine father, and last not least, a clear and emphatic recognition that this divine Fatherhood extends equally to the Gentile and the Jew. The second method of approximation is by increased loyalty to the fundamentals of our own faith, for thus we shall draw other communities nearer to ourselves. After all, the new theistic communities and the developments of old communities are new, and we as Jews have for our faith the most precious of all testimonies—the unbroken testimony of past generations. Our religion possesses all the picturesqueness, warmth, colour, poetry and romance which belongs to antiquity. Conduct based on the teaching of Judaism may attain to the sublime, and our lapses are due not to inherent defects in our faith, but to inherent defects in ourselves. The new organisations look to us for spiritual light. That light must be found burning with ever-increasing brightness in our own lives, and in the corporate life of our community. By loyalty to our own faith, and by reverent appreciation of the faith of other men, we shall help to establish the dominion of the God of love throughout the world.

THE END

www.ingramcontent.com/pod-product-compliance
Lightning Source LLC
Chambersburg PA
CBHW020431010526
44118CB00010B/522